Stress-Free S⸺⸺

Stress-Free Self-Publishing explains clearly the process you need to follow to publish your own book. It has easy to follow steps and walks you through all stages, giving pointers and recommendations along the way, drawing from Sam's many years of experience in this field. A must-read for any budding author struggling to get published. With this book at your side self-publishing is a reality. Thanks Sam for sharing your knowledge and experience.

Donna Neseyif, Baobab Growth

This book is a MUST-READ for any writer considering self-publishing their book. Not only does it take you through each step in great detail, the writer clearly knows the industry well and gives very useful tips to help you through the process, stress free. I will certainly be using this book page by page when I publish my business book.

Suzii Fido, Marketing with Ethics

An easy to understand guide to self-publishing. Suitable for both professional and amateur writers. Highly recommended for those considering writing or having written any type of book.

Martin Fido Marketing with Ethics

I would definitely recommend *Stress-Free Self-Publishing* as it has such valuable detailed insights about the publishing process and you feel like your hand is being held as you step through it, step by step.

Liz Almond, Insightful Minds

I absolutely love this book. It flows so easily and takes you through the process step-by-step in so much detail that you are in no doubt that you have all that you need to make it happen. A must-have guide for all self-publishing authors who want their book to be taken seriously.

Sheryl Andrews, Step by Step Listening

STRESS FREE FREE SELF PUBLISHING

HOW TO PUBLISH YOUR OWN BOOK
WITHOUT LOSING THE WILL TO LIVE

SAM PEARCE

Editing: Lexicon Marketing
Cover Design: Zeljka Kojic

Printed in the United Kingdom
First Printing, 2019

ISBN: 978-1-9160776-0-7 (Paperback)
ISBN: 978-1-9160776-1-4 (eBook)

SWATT Books Ltd.
Southampton, Hampshire
SO19 7QN

www.swatt-books.co.uk

Contents

Foreword

The world of publishing has evolved hugely in recent years and this has had both a positive and negative effect on publishers, authors and books. My own foray into the writing and publishing world was in 2009 when I started to write my first book, and this turned out to be an often bewildering and sometimes painful experience. It can be hard for even the most experienced author to make the right decisions for their book, let alone the novice! I spent many months seeking a traditional publisher, and although I had interest in my book, I eventually chose a different route. But I wasted a huge amount of time to get there. I wish I had known then what I know now!

Although there were many options back then, the industry has moved on hugely in the last ten years. There is still some negative press around self-publishing, but when done well, it provides a brilliant solution for any would-be author. I think it's great that technology has facilitated this change. Authors no longer have to wait for many months or even years to get their book published; it can now take just a few months to design, publish, distribute and sell a book worldwide.

There is a big problem though. With the many partnership and self-publishing options available for authors, it can be hard to find the best route for your book, and many feel overwhelmed with what to do next after they've written it. In addition, although it's easier than ever to get a book into the hands of your audience, there is a danger that this can be to the detriment of its quality and its impact.

So luckily there are people like Sam Pearce, who make it simpler for authors like you!

I met Sam in 2016, and it wasn't long before I realised that there was an easier and better way to get help to design and publish my books. I engaged Sam's services to publish my fifth book, *Book Marketing Made Simple*, and to create a second edition of *Your Book is the Hook*, and I loved what she did. So, I decided to work with Sam to help my clients to publish their books professionally.

I partnered with Sam and SWATT Books in January 2017, and she supports the publishing arm of Librotas Books. Her expertise lies in helping clients to ensure that the book that they've worked hard to write is published in a professional and aesthetically pleasing manner. This enables it to stand out and do what they wanted in the first place, which is most often to sell copies, build credibility and achieve greater business success.

On top of that, our clients don't need to worry about what to do and when, as Sam takes care of this. When most authors are an expert in their subject or genre, having someone take care of the publishing stuff makes it easier for them to focus on what they're good at.

I also appreciate that engaging a book mentor, a designer or publisher might be a financial step too far for some authors. They may wish to continue to do it themselves or to understand the process before they outsource the project, and that's where this book comes in.

Here, Sam breaks down the process of self-publishing into easy to manage chunks, so that you have no excuse but to produce a professional end-product. Whether you want to know how to find a good designer or to upload your book for sale, you'll get great tips and advice.

This book is a comprehensive, no-nonsense guide outlining the pitfalls and benefits of taking the self-publishing approach, with advice on what to do, who to use and screenshots to make it easy for you.

So, get stuck in, read this book and then get started yourself. Or if you want to do more of what you're good at, you can, of course, engage Sam to help you!

Karen Williams,
The Book Mentor, Librotas, supporting experts to write,
publish and market credibility and business building books.

Acknowledgements

Many people have helped me throughout the journey to publishing this book. Without the support and guidance that I received from them, I don't think this book would have finally made it into existence.

First and foremost, I would like to thank my loving husband, Nathan. Not only for putting up with having copies of the raw manuscript scattered around the house for months, but also for being so understanding when I decided to finish the initial writing of this book on a family holiday in Crete.

I also want to thank: Karen Williams for agreeing to write the foreword, and for keeping me accountable and on track throughout the later stages of the book. Sheryl Andrews for asking the tough questions and reminding me that I needed to follow my own advice when I got stuck. Louise Lubke Cuss for letting me pick her brains about editing and for her helpful insights into self-editing. My editor Mark Beaumont-Thomas for anglicising my Canadianisms, and for going above and beyond the call of duty to help me make this the best book it could be.

Finally, I would like to say a big thank you to all my peer reviewers, who helped me to make sure that this book would genuinely help those who are looking to self-publish. I know that most of you will be progressing with your own self-publishing journeys after this, and I sincerely hope that my book will support you along the way.

Chapter 1

Introduction to Self-Publishing

Hi there, and welcome to the world of self-publishing. In this book, I want to give you a solid grounding on what self-publishing is and isn't, as well as providing you with a clear and concise method of how to go about publishing your own book as easily and as stress-free as possible. I'm going to talk about some of the things you should consider before embarking on your self-publishing journey that will make the ride a little bit smoother, as well as some things you can do once your book is published to help make it more successful.

In the back of the book, I have also included a reference section that contains links to people, companies, and additional information to help you further.

One thing to note from the start is that this book assumes that you already have, or are well on your way to having, a completed first draft of your book written. This book does not touch on how to write or structure a book; mainly because that is not my area of expertise, but also because how you go about writing a good book differs fiction to non-fiction, genre to genre. If you want advice on how to write a book, there are hundreds if not thousands of books on the subject, as well as numerous online courses and coaches around the world who can help you. To get you started, I have listed the few that I can personally recommend in the references to.

The how-to section of this book contains screenshots to illustrate each step of the process for listing and publishing your book. Every effort has been made to make sure that these screenshots are as up-to-date as possible however technology evolves, and things change. To keep you up to date with the latest developments from the various publishing platforms that I discuss in this book, I have created an online resource where you can find full-size versions of all screenshots as well as additional tools and resources that you might find helpful. Please visit www.swatt-books.co.uk/SFSP to request access.

Who this book is for

I have written this book with four categories of author in mind. These categories bear no relationship to what 'type' of author you are in terms of what you write. Whether it be fiction, non-fiction, poetry or anthology, that doesn't matter. What does matter is where you are on your publishing journey. Regardless of what you write, there are four categories of author who will find this book useful: the Explorer, the Disillusioned, the Underdog, and the Renegade.

The Explorer
The Explorer will be just starting their journey as an author. They will be in the process of writing their first book and will be starting to think about how they are going to get that book into the hands of their readers. By their nature, Explorers tend to be fairly analytical; wanting to get all the facts and explore all the options before deciding on a course of action.

The Disillusioned
The Disillusioned have written their first book and have been trying to get it published through a traditional publisher without much success. They know that their book has a market, and has value to the readers within that market, but have become disillusioned trying to convince the publishing house gatekeepers of that fact, and so have decided to do it themselves.

The Underdog

The Underdog is an author who, like the Disillusioned, has written their first book, and has then published it themselves. However, for any number of reasons this first attempt didn't work as well as they hoped. Maybe they rushed into it without knowing what the process was. Or they felt at the time that they could do it all themselves without any support. Or maybe they just weren't able to put their full commitment behind it. But like a true fighter, the Underdog is not ready to give up and wants to give self-publishing another go, but this time by doing things correctly from the beginning.

The Renegade

Last but not least, the Renegade is the most experienced out of the four categories. They have a book or books already published by a traditional publisher but are not entirely happy with the experience. Perhaps the publisher hasn't entirely fulfilled their promises regarding marketing or distribution; maybe the book has gone through so many changes that it no longer feels like the book they wrote, or they're just not satisfied with earning 5% for all their hard work. For whatever reason, the Renegade has decided to rebel against the system and take back control of the publishing process.

If you can see aspects of yourself reflected in any or all of these four characterisations, then you are in the right place, and this book is going to help you achieve your publishing ambitions.

What is self-publishing?

In its purest form, self-publishing is when an author takes full ownership of the publishing process, either by doing it all themselves or hiring a professional or professionals to do the work on their behalf. This includes writing, editing, typesetting, design, cover art, pricing, publishing, marketing and PR.

By its nature, self-publishing gives full rights and ownership of the book to the author, as opposed to any other party. However, with the rights and ownership comes the responsibility for all the production costs associated with publishing that book. This can involve a considerable up-front investment as well as ongoing investment in marketing and PR activities, but the pay-off is that the author gets to keep 100% of the royalties earned from every copy sold.

In contrast, with the traditional publishing model, the responsibility for editing, design, publication and marketing lies with a publishing company (often referred to as a publishing house). They bear all of the initial publishing costs associated with getting a book to market. However, in return they will keep the lion's share of the royalties, with the author only receiving on average 5-10%. It is worth noting that in nearly all instances, the author will be required to sign over some or all of the rights to their book to the publisher as part of their book deal, and in some cases, this can even extend to future books the author writes. Despite this, traditional publishing has been the preferred choice for authors for the past century; mainly for the enticement of an advance or signing bonus that usually accompanies such book deals.

The lines between traditional publishing and self-publishing have become slightly blurred in recent years with the emergence of a third publishing option commonly known as hybrid publishing. In this model, an author will pay a lump sum to an online publishing service to have their book published. The publishing service will supply editing and design and will manage the publishing process of the book; often using the same methods as those used for self-publishing. All the author is required to do is market the book to generate sales. Sounds great, right? But there is a catch. In nearly all instances, the ISBN numbers assigned to your book will be owned by the publishing service, which means that without realising it you are still assigning certain rights for your book to the publishing service (namely ownership of the published book and copyright of the artwork). So even though you paid to have your book published, you are not much better off than if you signed a contract with a publisher. The only benefit is that they did the legwork for you, and you didn't have to go through the long and often painful process of pitching your book to a load of different publishing houses.

Reading that back to myself, I guess that my opinion of hybrid publishing is pretty obvious; I find the practices of many online 'book factory' hybrid publishers slightly immoral. They don't do anything more than what authors are able to do for themselves, yet they not only take a cut of the royalty for every book sold, they also retain rights to the book by taking advantage of many authors' limited understanding of ISBN numbers.

There are, however, exceptions to the rule. There is an elite level of hybrid publishers who genuinely earn the royalty commission they take in exchange for supporting authors in a way that they would not be able to do for themselves. A perfect example is that of Librotas Books, who offer book writing mentorship alongside their publishing. In many cases, books published by Librotas would never even have been written without the additional support that Karen and her team provides. And that is the key point of difference. If you are going to give up ISBN ownership and a portion of your royalties, make sure that what you get in exchange is worth it.

That aside, the decision as to which publishing option is right for you is a very personal one and is a decision that only you can make. That decision is one that has faced authors for much longer than you might think.

A history of self-publishing

Contrary to the popular belief that self-publishing is a recent phenomenon, self-publishing has been around since the invention of the printing press by Johannes Gutenberg in the 1400s. The printing press made it possible for writers with means to be able to pay printers to independently print their books as a form of rebellion against the establishment of Church and State. The earliest example of a self-published book that achieved notable success was *Tristram Shandy*, a two-volume satire by British writer Laurence Sterne in 1759[1]. Many well-known novelists at one point or another have chosen to self-publish or start their own presses. These include John Locke, Jane Austen, Emily Dickinson, Nathaniel Hawthorne, Martin Luther, Marcel Proust, Derek Walcott and Walt Whitman. However, the most famous example of early self-publishing success is the book *The Joy of Cooking*[2,3]. In 1931, Irma Rombauer, an amateur cook and suburban housewife, paid a local printer $3000 (half her life savings) to print 3,000 copies. With limited resources, Irma sold the book to her local community, and its reach expanded organically as word spread of its affordable, no-nonsense recipes and conversational style. After its initial success, the author produced an updated edition in 1936 and, after multiple rejections, publisher Bobbs-Merrill agreed to publish the book, which went on to become a bestseller with a total of eight editions, selling over 18 million copies worldwide.

Self-publishing success stories

Fifty Shades of Grey[4]

As well as Irma's book, there are many other notable self-publishing success stories; the most famous being that of the *Fifty Shades of Grey* trilogy by British

1   https://en.wikipedia.org/wiki/Self-publishing#Early_examples Accessed 3/03/2019

2   "The Joy of Cooking - Wikipedia." https://en.wikipedia.org/wiki/The_Joy_of_Cooking. Accessed 30 Jun. 2017.

3   "Irma S. Rombauer - Wikipedia." https://en.wikipedia.org/wiki/Irma_S._Rombauer. Accessed 30 Jun. 2017.

4   "Fifty Shades of Grey Author Interview E. L. James Before and After ...." 6 Feb. 2015, http://time.com/3697185/fifty-shades-of-grey-e-l-james-interview/. Accessed 30 Jun. 2017.

author EL James, which has sold 125 million copies in less than four years. The *Fifty Shades* trilogy started life as a serialised story called *Master of the Universe*, inspired by the Stephanie Myers vampire novel series *Twilight* that was posted on a Twilight fanzine. The author subsequently migrated it to her website, Fiftyshades.com, after comments questioning its explicit sexual nature. Sometime later she completely re-wrote it, removed it from her website and then self-published the first of three parts as an eBook. Shortly after, in May 2011, James released a print-on-demand paperback with the support of an independent Australian publishing house called The Writer's Coffee Shop. The 2nd and 3rd parts were also published by The Writer's Coffee Shop in September 2011 and January 2012 respectively. Due to the publisher's limited budget, marketing was restricted primarily to reviews by book bloggers and word of mouth marketing which, thanks to the particular demographic of its audience, soon went viral. Vintage Books bought the licence to the trilogy and quickly released a new and revised edition in April 2012. At the beginning of August of the same year, Amazon's UK arm announced that *Fifty Shades of Grey* had outsold the complete Harry Potter series in the UK.

The Martian[5,6,7]

The blockbuster Hollywood movie hit *The Martian,* which grossed over $600m at the box office, was also originally a self-published novel. *The Martian* was written by Andy Weir, a computer programmer and self-confessed space nerd, and was initially published in serial form on Weir's personal website, starting in 2009. Weir decided to take the self-publishing route with *The Martian* because literary agents had repeatedly turned down his earlier manuscripts. After numerous requests from readers to make the book available in its entirety, Weir published it in Amazon Kindle format in 2011 with a selling price of just 99 cents. The book quickly became an Amazon bestseller within the science fiction genre, selling in excess of 35,000 copies in less than a month. Its online popularity brought it to

5   "Adam Savage Interviews *The Martian* Author Andy Weir - The Talking ...." 11 Jun. 2015, https://www.youtube.com/watch?v=5SemyzKgaUU. Accessed 30 Jun. 2017.
6   "Andy Weir; the man whose space scribblings became *The Martian*." http://www.telegraph.co.uk/film/the-martian/andy-weir-author-interview/. Accessed 30 Jun. 2017.
7   "*The Martian* (Weir novel) - Wikipedia." https://en.wikipedia.org/wiki/The_Martian_(Weir_novel). Accessed 30 Jun. 2017.

the attention of numerous mainstream publishers, which resulted in deals first for an audiobook version in 2013 followed shortly afterwards by a publishing deal for a hardback version. The hardback version went on to achieve top twenty status on the New York Times bestseller list. As if all this wasn't enough, the film rights to the book were bought by 20th Century Fox and the film version, starring Matt Damon, was released in 2015.

The Celestine Prophecy[8]

The Celestine Prophecy is an immensely successful self-help book that explores the nature of humanity's connection to the divine, through a first-person narrative story of spiritual awakening written by James Redfield. Redfield self-published *The Celestine Prophecy* in 1992 under the imprint Satori Publishing, doing all the promotion, marketing and distribution himself, and selling more than 100,000 copies in two years. No mean feat given that the Internet was still in its infancy back then. Such was the book's popularity with readers and booksellers alike that Redfield was approached by Warner Books who bought the hardback rights to *The Celestine Prophecy* for $800,000 and went on to publish the first hardback edition in 1994. The book became a #1 bestseller in the US in 1996, selling more than 20 million copies worldwide.

Still Alice[9,10]

Still Alice by Lisa Genova is a perfect example of an author taking a manuscript rejected by traditional publishers and, with lots of hard work, turning it into a self-publishing fairy tale. Lisa's grandmother was diagnosed with Alzheimer's when she was in her 80s. As a result, the author witnessed first-hand as the disease "systematically disassembled the woman I knew as my grandmother." After researching the topic, Lisa discovered that most of the literature about this illness had been written by the clinicians or from the caregiver's point of view

8   "*The Celestine Prophecy* - Wikipedia." https://en.wikipedia.org/wiki/The_Celestine_Prophecy. Accessed 30 Jun. 2017.
9   "*Still Alice* (novel) - Wikipedia." https://en.wikipedia.org/wiki/Still_Alice_(novel). Accessed 30 Jun. 2017.
10 "Interview with Lisa Genova | ALZFORUM." http://www.alzforum.org/early-onset-familial-ad/profiles/interview-lisa-genova. Accessed 30 Jun. 2017.

rather than the patient's perspective. She wanted to understand what it felt like to have Alzheimer's from the first early symptoms onwards. After interviewing and working with many early-onset Alzheimer's patients, she wanted to find a way to share that understanding with others, and *Still Alice* was the answer. Genova self-published *Still Alice* as her first book in 2007, having spent a year unsuccessfully trying to interest literary agents in her manuscript. The last agent she saw warned her that self-publishing would kill her writing career before it had started, but thankfully for us all she ignored their advice and self-published using iUniverse. The way she tells it, "I was selling it out of the trunk of my car and trying to create a buzz." After a year of continuous guerrilla marketing techniques including Myspace, Goodreads and Shelfari, organising at least two book events every month and attending local book signings, her efforts started to pay off. At this point, she invested in a professional PR agent, and the resulting press and TV buzz led to her finding a sympathetic agent and subsequently lucrative audiobook and paperback deals. *Still Alice* then made it onto the New York Times bestseller list for over 40 weeks and has been translated into more than 20 languages.

Other successful self-published authors include[11]:

> Blogger Alan Sepinwall, whose book *The Revolution Was Televised* became an instant hit, winning a prominent review in the New York Times just two weeks after publication.

> Minnesota social worker Amanda Hocking published several books in 2010, and within a few months was earning enough money to quit her day job. She was awarded a lucrative book deal and then sold the rights to her series to St. Martin's Press in 2011 for £2m.

> Swedish author Carl-Johan Forssen Ehrlin became a bestseller with his book *The Rabbit Who Wants to Fall Asleep* which aims to aid parents with helping their child to fall asleep.

---

11 Self-Publishing success stories, Wikipedia. https://en.wikipedia.org/wiki/Self-publishing#Self-publishing_success_stories. Accessed 3/03/2019

> Erotic romance novelist Meredith Wild has sold 1.4m copies of her books after founding her own publishing company Waterhouse Press.

> The breakout sci-fi hit *Wool* by Hugh Howey was originally self-published and earned the author more the $1m in royalties and generated over 5000 Amazon reviews.

> James Altucher's book *Choose Yourself* sold over 44,000 copies in its first month, debuted at #1 on Amazon's non-fiction list, and went on to become a Wall Street Journal bestseller.

> Victoria Knowles's self-published book *The PA* achieved notoriety in July 2014 when it reached the #1 spot on the iTunes book chart for paid books.

Now I'm not going to lie to you; these books and authors are the exceptions as opposed to the rule, and success of this magnitude depends on a perfect storm of having the right book, at the right time, mixed with a lot of hard work. What all these success stories do have in common though is the unwavering belief from their authors that their book was worthy, and who then backed up that belief with an investment of both time and money to ensure that it became a success. So, if you believe in your book enough to invest in it, then you are on the right track.

Why self-publish?

I've covered quite a lot of ground already in terms of what self-publishing is, and I've touched on some of the reasons why many authors consider it a better way to publish in today's changing literary environment. But let me condense all those things down into a list of my top ten reasons why you should opt to self-publish your book.

1. Higher royalties

This is the obvious one and the reason you will see bandied around the most. But how much higher is 'higher'?

If you are lucky enough to get a book deal from a traditional publisher, and if you have a very good literary agent who is a star negotiator, you can get an advance of a couple of grand and between 10-15% of each book sold depending on your fan base and the 'clout' you bring to the table. 15-20% royalty is not unheard of. However, those sorts of rates are usually reserved for the JK Rowling's, Stephen King's, and James Patterson's of this world. But for an unknown author new to the game, you can expect to be offered an average of just 5-10% of your book's cover price.

Compare that with self-publishing where you can expect to earn between 50-70% of your cover price depending on the wholesale discount you offer. Achieving this sort of return does, however, require you to do your homework when setting a cover price, to ensure that it covers your production costs, with enough margin built in for both you and the bookseller while continuing to remain competitive.

2. Creative control

This is another popular reason that you will often hear.

When you sign a book deal with a traditional publisher, you are signing over the rights to your book. If during the editing process the in-house editor that the publisher has hired suggests changes to the book which you don't agree with –

tough luck. You can argue your case, but at the end of the day, it is the publisher's call. Same with cover design; the publisher may ask for your input, but as they are footing the bill for the designer, they have the final say. They will always opt for what is going to sell the largest number of copies, which may not always be what is best for the book.

With self-publishing, yes you pay for the editor and designer out of your own pocket. However, it will be a much more collaborative process because YOU are the paying client. Your opinion and what you want matters. Obviously, you will need to acknowledge that they are professionals and that you are hiring them for their expertise, but you retain greater control over the entire process.

3. Quicker to market

This is also a fairly common reason to self-publish, but one that is strangely not talked about as often.

The entire process of getting published in a traditional manner takes a long time, and you need to have the patience of a saint! Once you've written your book, you first need to find an agent. Then you need to go through the arduous process of pitching to publishers and waiting for the inevitable stream of rejection letters until a publisher finally decides to give you a chance. Only then can the actual editing and production process even start, but you are almost certainly not the only author which that publisher is managing at the time. Your book will be fed onto a conveyer belt of other books, running through a machine with lots of moving parts where any delay to any book in the chain will have a knock-on effect down the line. Consider yourself lucky if your book sees the light of day within a year!

Contrast that with self-publishing, where you can realistically expect to go from manuscript to on-sale in about 4-5 months. You can condense that timetable down a bit if you are prepared to shop around for editors and designers who can work to your schedule, but make sure you give them enough time to do their job properly.

Being quicker to market is especially beneficial to business authors looking to publish their books in conjunction with an event, as the lead-time to put on a professional event like a conference or trade show is probably about the same as self-publishing.

4. What you write has value to SOMEONE

This is an aspect of publishing that doesn't get talked about anything like as much as it should.

Traditional publishing is a numbers game. Even if you approach a publisher who specialises in books for a particular niche, the first question they are going to ask themselves when evaluating your book proposal is, "How many people will buy this book?" If the answer isn't at least five figures, they are unlikely to give your book further consideration. They are in the business of selling books, and generally don't care about whether your story "needs" to be told.

Because self-publishing has no gate-keepers, if you want to write about collecting fluffy pink unicorns, and you know that there are other people out there who also collect fluffy pink unicorns, then what you have to say has value. The only gatekeeper is you and your ability to reach that ultra-niche of readers. That is why knowing your market and having a marketing plan in place to get in front of them is so important if you are going to self-publish.

5. A more positive experience

Let's face it - at some point in every author's journey, you are going to be racked with feelings of doubt. The dreaded question, "Is my writing good enough?", has kept awake at 3am even the most successful authors somewhere along the way. So why would you want to bombard yourself with more doubt and negativity from the outside world? But that is exactly what you will face when you embark on finding a traditional publisher. You need to be willing to face dozens of rejection letters until you find a publisher willing to give you a shot. Even JK Rowling had the first *Harry Potter* book rejected 12 times before Bloomsbury signed it for an advance of just £1,500.

However, if you self-publish, the only opinions you need to worry about are the ones that matter most – yours and those of your readers. As long as you think in the same way as a publisher and invest in professional editing, peer review, and take the time to do your research, your book will be judged by what you have to say and not how you say it.

As an aside, if you do find yourself wrestling with questions of doubt during your writing journey, I highly recommend having a chat with Sheryl Andrews from Step by Step Listening; she has a fantastic programme to help authors manage their critic.

6. Not tied to a long-term contract

Very few authors take into consideration the length of time that their book will be tied to a traditional publisher when first looking to get a book deal. When you take into account how much of your book you are signing away, it's a very important factor to consider. It's not uncommon for publishing contracts to remain in effect for the life of the author plus the term of the copyright (which is 70 years in most territories). This means that your heirs will potentially be tied to that contract too!

With self-publishing, providing you purchase in your own name the ISBN numbers used in the publishing of your book, that ownership issue disappears. ISBN numbers do not expire and are not transferrable to another publication. So, once you have registered a book against an ISBN number with the governing ISBN agency for your territory, your book is yours to do with as you wish for the term of the copyright. After which, you (or your heirs) can request to extend the term if necessary.

7. Flexibility to change anything anytime

A secret fact about being an author that no one tells you about is that a book is never finished! Even if you are fortunate enough not to discover a typo staring you in the face when you open your freshly printed book for the first time, there are always improvements and changes to be made. Your book may hit the bestseller list, or you win a prestigious prize that you want to proudly emblazon on your front cover. Or perhaps new information comes to light or you change your opinion on a specific topic in your book, and so you want to update it. If you are tied to a traditional publisher for that book, you are obliged to go through all the red tape and argue your case as to why the book needs a second edition. Should you win the battle and the publisher agrees with you, the production process starts all over again.

On the other hand, if you self-publish that book, you or your designer simply make the amendments and resubmit the artwork. In the case of a full-on second edition, you just assign a new set of ISBN numbers out of the batch you purchased and repeat the listing process.

8. It's the biggest share of the book market and growing

It's common knowledge that the self-publishing segment of the book market is growing year on year and has been for the past decade. But what you may not know is that we are reaching a tipping point in the market share of self-published books versus those published by the 'Big 5' publishing houses such as Penguin and Random House. In some market segments, that market share has already tipped into self-publishing's favour. According to the January 2018 report by AuthorEarnings.com, the market share for self-published eBooks in the United States hit 45.7%, significantly outstripping the Big 5 publishing houses, whose share was a mere 25.6%. Overall sales growth of self-published books also increased more than for traditionally published books. Self-published sales increased by 2.1% in the final nine months of 2017 compared to 1.1% for traditional publishing.

9. Leverage to secure a book deal

If after reading everything up to this point you still want to secure a traditional publishing deal, then work the system in your favour! In recent years, traditional publishers have become wise to the potential of self-publishing. Many publishing houses now scout the bestseller lists, looking for indie authors who appear to be the next big thing. When publishers find them, they then approach authors direct, safe in the knowledge that the book has already proven itself. *Wool, Fifty Shades of Grey* or *The Martian* ring any bells?

This odd role reversal then puts the author firmly in the driver's seat when it comes to negotiating the best terms for a publishing contract. You now have something that the publisher wants; just make sure you are smart about what you ask for in return and always, always, ALWAYS have a contracts lawyer review any agreement before you sign on the dotted line.

10. Readers don't care

This last reason is one that most of the book industry, traditional and self-published, overlooks - the average reader doesn't care who the publisher is!!! If you were to ask a Game of Thrones fan who George RR Martin's publisher is, they probably wouldn't know. Even I had to look up that it was Harper/Voyager, and I've read the series umpteen million times! All the reader really cares about is that the book they are investing time and money to read is worth that investment. Is it well written? Is it easy to read? Is it entertaining or imparting some level of value or knowledge? That is all that matters.

So now that you know what self-publishing is and what its benefits are to you as an author, let's get into how you should go about getting your book published. Starting with making sure you are in the right mindset to achieve publishing success.

Chapter 2

Before you Start

As with any major project, writing and publishing a book can be a long and arduous process. Knowing what resources you will need, and most importantly WHY you are doing it and WHO you are doing it for, is going to help make the journey that little bit easier.

So, let's take a look at what you should consider and/or do before you get started, beginning with your mindset.

Mindset

Every successful achievement begins with having the right mindset from the very beginning. No matter how well you plan, you are going to encounter challenges and setbacks along your journey to becoming a published author. Having the right mindset won't prevent those setbacks, but it will help you cope with them and move on more quickly and easily.

First of all, you need to know your WHY. Why are you writing this book? Do you want to leave a lasting legacy? Are you fulfilling a lifelong ambition? Or do you want to pass on years of knowledge and experience to the next generation?

Knowing your why is vitally important to actually finishing your book. But most importantly, your why needs to be YOURS. If you are writing this book for someone else's reasons, then you will struggle to maintain motivation when the journey gets tough.

Once you know your why, the second aspect of mindset you need to get right is your approach; HOW you go about the process of writing and publishing your book. The best piece of advice that I have been given is to approach your book like a business; even if you are writing a novel or memoir. Treating your book like a business will make you look at all the angles and will help you to put a plan in place, not just for writing and publishing your book, but also for selling and marketing it afterwards.

I would even take this so far as to write a short business plan for your book. There are loads of great examples of one-page business plans out there that will help you gain clarity on some of the fundamentals in order to set the groundwork for your book's business journey.

Publishing plan

I appreciate that there may be some first-time authors reading this book who have never run their own business, so the idea of writing a business plan may be a bit alien. To help you out I'm going to break down the necessary steps you need to think about to put together a rough publishing (or book) plan. For those of you who have run your own businesses before and are familiar with business plans, this may help you adjust your thinking slightly from "business" to "book".

Every business plan in its rawest form serves to answer the 6 fundamental questions of **Who, What, Why, Where, When** and **How**. It is also beneficial to answer these questions in a defined order, as the answer to one often leads to the next question.

Who

An essential aspect of the business plan for your book is being clear about who you are writing for. Narrowing down your readership will help you to tailor your language when writing your book as well as targeting your marketing efforts once your book has been published. The more specific you can be the better. Think about general demographics such as age, gender, socio-economic position and education, but then go deeper than that.

Many authors will build an avatar of their ideal reader, assigning them a name, what they do for work, as well as hobbies, children, even down to where they live.

Now I know what you might be thinking – "Won't I be ruling out loads of potential readers?" The answer is no. You're not preventing anyone from buying or reading your book. What you are doing is targeting your book to the readers who will enjoy it the most or get the most out of it. In order for you to target those readers effectively, you need to know as much about them as possible.

Where

Now that you know who your reader is, you next need to think about where you will go to find them (i.e. where are you going to market your book?). If you happen to be your own target market, answering this question is relatively straightforward – where do you hang out or search for information or inspiration? If you are not your target audience, then you need to do a little bit of market research and delve into where you can find your audience most frequently. Is it on Facebook, or are they more face-to-face type people? Will they be more receptive in a business type of environment like LinkedIn, or will they find that too "corporate" and prefer to flick through Instagram or Pinterest?

Knowing where your reader is going to be will form the basis of where you target your marketing efforts. This is crucial if you are going to be marketing your book on a budget and can't afford to plaster your book's name everywhere.

Why

The next question you need to ask yourself is "Why?" Why will your reader choose to read your book over another? In business circles, this is known as your USP or Unique Selling Point/Proposition. What makes your book different? What makes you uniquely qualified to be writing this book? Why should your readers care? On the surface, these questions can seem a bit obvious and possibly even a little naive, but if you really put yourself into your readers' shoes when thinking about these questions, it will make your book more focused. Also, the answers to these questions will help make your marketing easier to undertake effectively, because these answers will form the basis of any key marketing messages that will resonate with your target audience.

What

Once you are able to answer questions of who, where and why, you need to ask yourself What... What do you want out of publishing your book? Some people may find this question a little selfish, but you are the one who is going to be putting countless hours, days, weeks, months, possibly even years into writing and publishing your book; you should be getting something out of this commitment.

There are several answers to this question, such as recognition, credibility, enhancing your profile, additional income or even a new career path. It can even be multiple answers. The important thing to remember is that any answer only really pertains to you, and like your why, will help you to maintain focus and motivation when challenges arise.

When

Another fundamental question to answer that many authors get stuck on is When... when do you need your book published? It's very important to be realistic here; self-publishing in a proper manner takes time, but how much time?

If you are reading this book before you have completed (or started) writing your manuscript, you first need to take into account how long it will take you to write your book. Here you need to be very honest with yourself as to how much time you can realistically dedicate to your writing, and also how you write. If writing comes naturally to you and you find you can get into the flow easily, then you might be able to dedicate short bursts every day. If, however, you struggle to get going then it will be more beneficial to you to dedicate large chunks of time to your writing; maybe even take a writing retreat so that you can concentrate on your book for an entire weekend or even a week.

I combined both tactics in the writing of this book. I started out dedicating entire afternoons once a week to writing to get into the swing of it as I hadn't done any considerable writing since I was in grade school in Canada. Once I got back into the habit of writing regularly, I started writing short snippets every day over my morning coffee. After I gave myself a deadline of when I wanted the book finished, I took my manuscript on holiday with me in spring 2018 and spent the week putting the finishing touches to it ready for editing.

Once you have your book written, you then need to factor in how long it's going to take to publish. Every book is going to be different, but on average you should anticipate that the publishing of your book, from the moment you hand your manuscript to an editor to being on sale, will take 4-5 months. Each stage of the process needs time to be completed effectively. To give you an idea of how long each taste can take, on the next page is a screenshot of a standard book production schedule that I give to my clients. It lists all of the various tasks that need to be completed and the order in which they will happen, including who is responsible for each task. Some tasks may take longer, some may be completed ahead of schedule, so this sort of timeline can shift as a book progresses, but it will give you an idea of what to expect.

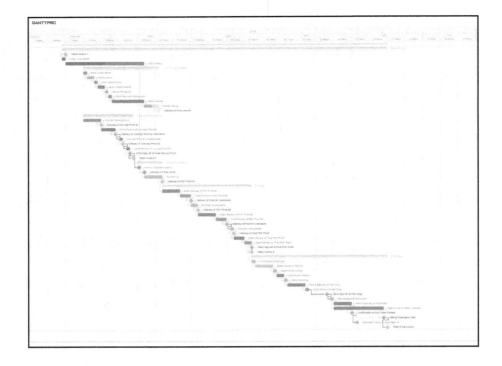

I would strongly recommend putting together a schedule for yourself and holding yourself accountable to deadlines. It is very easy to put off things that don't have a fixed deadline attached to them. I found this when writing this book; when I started, I worked on it when I had some spare time (and spare motivation); but I wasn't rigorous about it. However, as soon as I gave myself a concrete date of when I wanted (needed) the book published, things progressed at a consistent pace. It helped that I linked my deadline to an event beyond my control (*Trainer Talk Live* in May 2019) and asked the organiser if I could launch the book alongside my keynote speech. This meant that it wasn't just my arbitrary deadline I was working to, but a deadline that was controlled by someone else who was relying on me to deliver. It acts as a tremendous motivator!

How

Finally, you need to think about How. How actually breaks down into two separate questions, and these are:

> How much will it cost?
> How do I actually do it?

How much will it cost?

A vital part of your planning should be working out a realistic budget. It is possible to self-publish a book completely for free; however, if you want your book to be successful and credible, you need to invest in doing it properly. But how much money will you need?

First off, you should purchase your own ISBN numbers. There are many self-publishing platforms out there that give you the option of using their ISBN numbers, but don't be fooled by this as you will be giving up more than you will save. **Owning the ISBN number assigned to your book means you retain 100% of the legal rights over your book.** Whereas if you have used an ISBN number assigned to you by a hybrid publisher or a self-publishing platform, while you will have retained creative copyright over the content of the book, legally the physical book will now belong to them, not you. At the time of publication, a block of 10 ISBN numbers from Nielsen's (the ISBN agency for the UK and Ireland) costs £185. More about ISBN numbers later.

Secondly, you want to invest in a good editor. No matter how good you are at writing or at English, it can always be improved. Plus, it's very easy to miss errors in your own writing, as your brain knows what it has meant to say and becomes blind to mistakes. The next chapter will go into editing in more detail, but as a rough budget, set aside around £500-£750 for editing, depending on the length and nature of your manuscript.

Next you need to earmark some funds to hire a professional designer; ideally to create your cover and book interior, but at the very least to design your cover art. Chapter Four is dedicated to book design and why it is important, but for now allocate £500-£2000; £500 for cover art only, and up to £2000 for a complete book design and typesetting package.

There are varying levels of cost when it comes to the actual publishing of your book, depending on what method of self-publishing you are planning on pursuing. If you are planning on releasing a simple eBook, there is just a $25 listing fee from Ingram Spark (see page 64 for more info on Ingram Spark). If you are planning on releasing your book as a print-on-demand title, then you will need to factor in the cost of having a stock of books printed for your own sales fulfilment and marketing purposes. These costs are purely governed by the print specification of your book, which won't be finalised until the later stages of the process. However, you need to be aware of these costs and make sure you have some funds available. A good way to get a rough idea is to take a look at the print specification of similar books in your genre and then input those into the print and shipping calculator on Ingram Spark's website. It won't be exact, but it will give you a good start-point.

If, however, you are planning on self-distributing your book, the costs involved can be very high. You will need to order print copies of your book from a traditional printer, who will insist on a minimum order quantity. You will also need to factor in the storage costs of those books and distribution charges for getting your books from your storage to retailers. Add on top of that the need for a wholesale distributor if you want to distribute your book any wider than your local area, and the costs can start to really rack up.

Lastly, have a think about what sort of marketing you would like to do for your book and set aside funds as appropriate. There are no hard and fast rules as to what marketing you should do, as long as you do something. It can be anything from Facebook ads to Goodreads giveaways (look at www.goodreads.com), to a full-blown launch party. The possibilities are endless, from completely free to thousands of pounds. My recommendation is that if your budget is limited, start with low cost/no cost options to build initial momentum, and then look to invest a portion of book sales into a larger marketing campaign once your book gains some traction. More about marketing in Chapter Six.

So, in answer to the question, "How much does it cost to self-publish a book?" the answer can be, "As much as you want it to cost." Realistically though, as a rough guideline, you will need to budget around £3,000 from start to finish. But remember that every book is different and therefore every budget can be different too. My advice is as soon as you have a rough idea of how long your book is going to be, start talking to professional editors and designers and get some estimates. That way you can start fine-tuning your plan and your budget as necessary.

How do I do it?

Now that you know who your book is for, why you're writing it, and what you're going to need to make it happen, you can get to work. However, any journey is easier when you know the route, so the final thing you should do before you start is to familiarise yourself with the process. This is what the rest of this book focuses on – the process of how to self-publish a book.

There are six main phases to self-publishing a book:

1. Writing

2. Editing

3. Book design and typesetting

4. Setting yourself up as a self-publisher

5. Publishing your book

6. Marketing - launch and ongoing

As I've mentioned before, there are hundreds (if not thousands) of books, courses, mentor groups and coaches out there that focus on how to write a book, but that's not what this book is about. We're going to pick things up from the point where you have completed your first draft manuscript.

Are you ready? Let's get started…

Chapter 3

Editing

It is vital that you understand that your book is an investment – not only of your time but financially as well. In order to give your book the best chance of success, there are aspects where it is in your best interest to open your cheque book and hire a professional, and editing is by far the most important one.

Why editing is important

Nothing puts a reader off more than a book that is full of spelling and grammatical errors, inconsistencies, or just doesn't flow well. You can be telling the most compelling story or imparting knowledge that will change the reader's life, but if the reader can't see past the language to the content, then it's all for nothing.

"I don't need an editor, I'm great at English"

I hear this from authors and clients all the time, and I'm here to tell you that no matter how good your spelling and grammar is, or how well you did in English at school, every author needs an editor. I know Rhodes scholars and university professors of English Lit that swear by their editors. The reason for this is that book editing is about so much more than just checking for spelling mistakes.

As an author, you have lived and breathed your manuscript for months, maybe even years; you KNOW what you are trying to say. However, writing a book involves high-level brain functions such as turning ideas and concepts into complex sentences, that your brain tends to dedicate less attention to the lower level functions, such as turning thoughts into words. There are numerous studies and research experiments that have been conducted on this subject, including a psychology study at the University of Sheffield, and they all come to similar conclusions. No matter how smart you are, it is very difficult to spot your own mistakes, because what you read on the paper/screen is competing with the version that is in your head. An editor will be reading your book with completely fresh eyes. Not having the foreknowledge of what you are trying to say, they will be able to read exactly what is written and proofread it accordingly.

There is another reason why you need an editor that is related to your familiarity with your subject, and that is checking understanding. This is particularly important for non-fiction authors. You are probably writing about a topic that you are intimately familiar with as an expert in your field. What may seem simple and easy to you may prove to be very difficult for a layman to understand, as they won't have the benefit of your background, experience or expertise. In these instances, it is very easy to gloss over points that your reader needs more information about to fully understand the topic. An editor will be reading your book from the standpoint of your audience, but without your knowledge or background behind them. The editor can then point out areas that need more explanation in order to be clear.

Three types of editing

Now that you understand why editing is so important, it's important to understand that there are several different types of editing. The more levels of editing you apply to your book, the better it will be for it, but of course sometimes budgets don't allow for that. So, I'm going to break down the various levels of editing for you so that if you do need to watch the pennies, you can decide which ones you need and which you can potentially skip.

Developmental editing

This is the most intensive form of editing and should be done once you have completed your first rough draft. It looks more at WHAT you are saying as opposed to HOW you are saying it. Your book is evaluated as a whole for problems with structure, organisation, coherence and logic. This form of editing can often result in fairly radical changes being suggested in terms of entire sections being rewritten, moved, deleted or added.

Copy editing

Copy editing starts to look at HOW you are writing and aims to correct problems with grammar, style, repetition, word usage and jargon. This is usually applied to the final draft manuscript before it is sent to a designer for typesetting.

Proofreading

This is the lightest form of editing and should ideally be performed after the manuscript has been typeset. Please check with your designer that at least one round of artwork changes is included, or this could cost you extra - more on this subject later. This is where the editor drills down to basics and corrects minor errors such as verb tenses, spelling, punctuation, capitalisation and the consistency of the expression of items such as titles and numbers.

Why hire a pro and what to consider

If you don't already have an editor, it can be quite daunting looking for one, as there is a lot of choices available and not everyone who claims to be an editor is fit to edit your book. So, what should you be looking for?

First question to ask is if they have experience in editing books, as opposed to just websites or corporate brochures. Though the basic process may be the same, editing a full-length book is a far more intensive process than a website and encompasses a much broader subject to review for consistency. Make sure they are up to the task.

Second is their working methodology. Most good editors will work with 'Track Changes' in Word for manuscripts, and Annotated PDFs for final post-typeset proofreading. Discuss with them whether their way of editing works for you and what you can expect to receive back from them. Check whether they will send you changes for you to review and apply, or if they will send you revised copy with changes already made.

Next, enquire as to their availability and whether it fits your publishing schedule. Obviously, you need to be realistic here; editing – especially more intensive developmental editing – is a time-consuming process. So, allow enough time for your editor to do their job properly without being rushed. But be aware that many editors will only work on one or two books at a time so you may need to schedule their time in advance.

Consider whether familiarity with your subject is necessary. Some editors specialise in only fiction or non-fiction. But beyond that, especially for highly specialised non-fiction topics, the editor may require some background knowledge of your subject in order to edit your book effectively. If your book does require a specialised editor, don't be afraid to ask other authors in your industry who they used. Also look at the verso (copyright) pages or the acknowledgements sections of similar books as many editors receive credit for their work.

As with buying any service, look for someone with good testimonials, and don't be afraid to get in touch with some of the people providing the testimonials to ask their opinion of working with that editor. Because no matter how good someone is at their job, if they are a nightmare to work with, it's rarely worth it.

Lastly, and only if you have considered all the previous points, do you consider the price. When it comes to editing, it is a false economy to compromise on any of the above considerations in the hope of paying a cheaper rate. Your book, and by extension your success and credibility, will suffer in the long run.

I appreciate that all this is a lot to consider and it can be a bit overwhelming, but it is important to find someone who ticks all of those boxes. A great place to start is with the Society for Editors and Proofreaders (SfEP – www.sfep.org.uk). They are a professional organisation based in the UK for editors and proofreaders. Members of the SfEP are obliged to adhere to a strict level of standards and agree to be held to a code of practice to ensure editorial excellence. They also have a fantastic online directory of more than 700 members which is fully searchable by skills, subject, location and services offered.

How you can help

There are several ways that you can help to make your editor's job easier. First and foremost is to perform a self-edit. The more polished your book is before it goes to the editor, the less work they need to do and therefore the less it will cost you. There are loads of free resources and advice online to help you out if you've never edited a long document before, but here are a few tips to get you started:

> **Take a break first.** Take at least a week (ideally more if you have the time) away from your book. Don't read it, don't work on it and don't even think about it. That way when you come back to it, your brain has had a chance to forget the words that you have written, allowing you to read it fresh.

> **Read out loud or use text-to-speech software.** Listening and reading use different parts of the brain. What you hear out loud can be different from what you hear in your head when reading a piece of text; especially one that you have written. This technique can help you to pick out sentences or phrases that are a bit clunky. If you get tongue-tied trying to say it, then it's likely that your reader will find it difficult to read or understand.

> **Segregate problem passages.** When you do find a sentence or phrase that just doesn't quite work, try copying and pasting it into a blank document and work on it in isolation.

> **Be mindful of your language usage.** Avoid unnecessary jargon, and if you do need to use technical terminology and jargon, then think about including a jargon buster. This will also help improve your readers' experience as well as that of your editor. If your editor doesn't understand a term and needs to ask you for clarification, it's likely that your reader won't either. The exception to this is obviously technical books aimed at an audience with a certain level of pre-understanding. In this instance, you would look for an editor who also has an understanding of the topic to avoid unnecessary queries about specific words or phrases.

The next thing you can do to help your editor is to tidy up the formatting. In-depth editing can be much more mentally draining and taxing on the eyes than just reading, and there are a few really simple techniques you can employ that will make your book easier for your editor to work on:

> Increase your line spacing to at least 1.5-2.0
> Remove any double spaces at the end of sentences
> Ensure that similar sections and content types have the same formatting

The final thing you can do that will help keep your editing bills to a minimum is to do your homework. Make sure that any quotes or references from external sources (no matter how small) are correctly attributed. This applies to printed material as well as information from the Internet, speeches, talks and lectures. This not only saves your editor from having to look up missing references and check their accuracy, but it is also a legal requirement.

Ensure that any requests for permissions that may be needed are well underway before you get to the editing stage. Getting permission to use other people's work in your book as early as possible avoids the potential for lengthy rewrites and doubling up of editing work later on.

Peer review

The last point that I want to touch on in terms of editing is the idea of peer review. This is very prevalent in the academic community, in particular in scientific and medical research papers and is starting to become more popular in trade book publishing. Before a paper is published, a panel of other scientists or doctors from the same field review it for credibility. Now I'm not suggesting that you give a copy of your book to your competitor to tear apart, but I believe the concept has a great deal of merit in the wider publishing industry. In fact, the idea of ARCs (Advance Reader Copies) is starting to grow in popularity.

Giving a copy of your book to trusted peers within your industry or to influential members of your target audience prior to publication can be invaluable. Not only can they catch any last-minute errors, but they can also provide important feedback on its content. It can also be a powerful marketing strategy to build buzz about your book prior to its release.

It is very important to note that if you are going to engage in peer review, it should be done at a particular point within the editing process. Ideally you should send your book out for peer review AFTER any developmental editing has been completed, but BEFORE your manuscript goes off for line editing. This is to ensure that any major changes that affect the way the book reads have been made so that your reviewers get a true sense of your book, but also gives you the opportunity to apply any changes that are suggested by your reviewers before line editing. If you then make changes to your manuscript after editing, you could very easily introduce new errors into the book which then require a second round of paid editing.

Peer review is a valuable exercise to engage in - however, it can be a bit scary for some authors. This is generally the first time you will be sending your book to anyone other than yourself (or maybe a partner) to read. I know of many authors who have opted out of conducting a peer review due to the fear of judgement or rejection before their book is even finished. And I fully get it... I sent this book out for peer review and I can vividly remember that it took me over an hour to click send on the five emails that I had drafted asking people to review my book.

However, I can attest that it has been well worth the discomfort. As soon as I did click send, I found myself more excited about the book than I had been in the weeks leading up to that day. I also feel that the feedback that I received has led me to publish a better book than it would have been without that advice and constructive criticism.

One word of caution that I would give in regard to engaging in peer review is to think carefully about who you ask to review your book. Be mindful to choose people who will be both honest and supportive, but who are willing to give you constructive criticism if it is needed. Also be sure to select people who are your target audience. There is no point getting someone to review your book if they are not going to be interested in it or understand it. So, by all means ask your mum to read your book, but if she's not your target audience then weigh her feedback accordingly. ☺

Chapter 4

Book Design

So you have your manuscript finished and edited to perfection. Now it's time to turn it into an actual book. This is another one of those areas where you want to invest in a professional, in this case a book designer. At the very least you need them to design the cover, and if you can stretch to it, to typeset the contents too. Similar to editing, you don't want to cut corners in order to save a few quid, because ultimately your book's design can make the difference between it selling and not.

Why book design is so important

I have written numerous articles on why book design is important and how it can impact on your book's success. But let's break it down in terms of the impact design has on each stage of the journey a reader will take with your book.

Getting noticed

We've all heard the saying, "Don't judge a book by its cover". However, that is exactly what most people do with a book by an author they haven't heard of before. So as a new author, shelf appeal is of utmost importance. Your book needs to stand out as one that is worth readers' time and attention. It needs to express one of two things instantly: either it must convey exactly what the book is about so that the reader knows whether it is for them; or it needs to generate enough curiosity to make the reader pick it up to see what it is all about.

In today's world of mass media overcommunication, it takes a skilled designer to be able to utilise the limited canvas of a book cover in such a way that it communicates all those things clearly and concisely within the split-second timeframe that your book has to make an impression. Only a skilled designer has the background and understanding of colour psychology, layout hierarchy, typography and image manipulation to create a cover which will elicit the emotional response from a reader that will make them pick up your book from the shelf.

Buying decision

Now that the reader has your book in their hand, the design and content need to work in partnership to get you over the finish line and convince the reader to buy your book. The first thing everyone does when they pick up a book for the first time is turn it over and read the back. What you write in your synopsis is vitally important in converting the sale, but it is your designer's job to present that synopsis in a clear, easy to read and accessible format (see more about writing a synopsis on page 68). How things like bullet points, callouts and testimonials are designed and typeset all have an impact on the reader's decision as to whether your book is right for them.

If your book passes the back cover test, 95% of people will quickly skim through the contents; probably leafing through pages and possibly stopping briefly if something catches their eye. This is where professional page layout and typesetting start to play their part. During this cursory flick through, the reader is not going to read enough of the content to be influenced by what you have to say. However, their brain will be making all sorts of subconscious decisions about your book based on how it is laid out. Is the text easy to read and therefore easy to understand? Is the layout clean and professional and therefore a credible source of information? Are the chapters and headings clear and therefore less effort to read? If it's a novel, does the typography convey a sense of the story and therefore build interest? All of these thoughts and more will be going through the reader's mind as they skim through your book, and it takes a designer with excellent typographical knowledge to be able to lay out and typeset your book so that the answers to all of those various questions are in your favour and ultimately lead to a sale.

Reader experience

Congratulations! You've won the bookstore battle and the reader is going home with your book in their hand, ready to start reading it. Now your writing has a chance to shine, all the while being supported by the design. This is where a professional designer really makes a difference. Great book typesetting has a number of important jobs to do while being as unobtrusive and invisible as possible.

Font choice needs to be such that the text is easy to read. Paragraph formatting and page layout need to ensure that the reader doesn't suffer fatigue or headaches if reading for long periods of time. In the case of non-fiction, information needs to be presented in a way that is easy to understand and possibly cross-referenced at a later date. Any images, charts or graphs need to be integrated seamlessly in order to not interrupt the reader's flow.

All of these things will have a subtle yet profound impact on the reader's overall impression of your book. Get any one of the elements wrong, and there is a chance that the reader won't even make it to the end. Whether the overall impression you leave with the reader is really good or really bad, it may well prompt them to post a review of your book, which could make a huge impact on the buying decision of the next reader. Which starts the cycle all over again.

Benefits of outsourcing a designer

Hopefully, from that walk through of the buying process, you can see how important the design of your book is. Now think about it from the point of view of all the minute decisions you need to make when designing your book in order to influence those various aspects of the buying process. To really drive this point home, here is a list of decisions that a designer needs to make during the course of an average book project – and note that this list is far from exhaustive:

> Trim size
> Black & white or full colour
> Body copy font
> Body copy weight
> Body copy size
> Heading font
> Heading weight
> Heading size
> Subheading font
> Subheading weight
> Subheading size
> Line length
> Margin width
> Bullet point treatment
> Numbered list treatment
> Quote treatment
> Pull box design

> Embedded or inline images?
> Image selection/quality
> Chart/graph design
> Colour choice
> Page furniture placement
> Indexing
> Table of contents
> Cross referencing
> Footnotes/endnotes
> PDF export settings
> Bleed requirements
> Chapter plates
> External hyperlinks
> Leading/kerning
> Widows & orphans
> Line/paragraph/page breaks
> Baseline grid

I don't mean to create even more overwhelm for you, and I'm well aware that there are technical words and phrases in that list which may well mean nothing to you, but the length of that list illustrates why I strongly recommend that you engage a professional designer to help you design and typeset your book. They will have the experience, understanding and training to be able to make all of those decisions to come up with the optimum design for your book to match the needs of your prospective readers.

Finding a designer

Now that I have convinced you of how important design is to the success of your book, what should you look for when hiring a designer?

First of all, you want to look through their portfolio at other books they have designed. Counter-intuitively, you want to look for a designer who doesn't have a set style to their work. Even if your subject matter has been written about before, your book is unique. You don't want a designer who will take a cookie-cutter approach. Ask them if they use set templates or if they will present concepts developed specifically for your book and make sure the answer is the latter.

Opt for a designer who offers an initial consultation before you are obliged to commit to using them. This is beneficial for various reasons. Writing a book is a highly personal thing; you want to make sure that you have a good rapport with your designer and feel you can trust them. You also want to get a sense of how collaboratively they work and how receptive they are to your ideas. A good designer will want to work closely with you and will understand that while they are the professional, at the end of the day it is your book.

As with choosing an editor, you want to look at any testimonials the designer has received, and if possible, get in touch with a few of their past clients. Enquire as to the level of success their books have had.

Before committing to a particular designer, go through their proposal and T&Cs very carefully. Take note of how many revisions are included in each stage of the book's development, and exactly what is and isn't included in the fee (such as stock photography purchases or the number of proofs). Also, make sure there aren't any restrictions on artwork ownership or copyright.

If you have a specific deadline by which you want your book published, be sure to make the designer aware of this and ask that they put together a project schedule for you so that you are both aware of timescales and deadlines for key milestones.

Lastly, you ideally want to look for a designer who has experience with eBook conversions. So often I see eBooks on Kindle or iBooks that bear no resemblance to their print counterparts. But if you can find a designer who knows their way around HTML and CSS code and how they relate to eBooks, there is no reason why the eBook and print editions of your book can't be in perfect harmony with each other. More on this topic later in the chapter.

BONUS: It can be extremely advantageous in the long run if you are able to find a book designer who also offers self-publishing management. This means that for an additional fee they can help guide you through the rest of the self-publishing process. Again, do your research into previous books where they have assisted in the publishing to make sure that they do know what they are doing, and ensure you are clear on exactly what is and isn't included in their fee.

Outsourcing vs DIY

I fully appreciate that some authors just cannot afford to outsource the design and typesetting of their entire book. Hopefully, I have convinced you that if you can you should, but I also want to help if you can't.

If you need to do your design and typesetting yourself, please consider these tips:

> **Be ruthless in regard to consistency**
Make sure that every instance of a particular type of text is formatted EXACTLY the same way. Use style sheets to help you with this.

> **Consider purchasing a template**
There are ready-made templates that you can purchase to use as a base for your book. Be mindful that this approach will mean your book will not be unique, but it can act as a great starting point if you are not a Word or Adobe InDesign expert.

> **Learn as much as you can**
>
> Trawl through resources like Udemy and YouTube to find tutorial videos that will help you to make your formatting look as professional as possible.

After the publication of this book, I will be putting together an online DIY course to support authors who wish to learn more in-depth techniques for book design and self-publishing. Be sure to register for access to the online resource that accompanies this book and to be kept up-to-date on when this course will be launching: www.swatt-books.co.uk/SFSP.

Timing

I strongly recommend that you engage a designer at the same time as you send your draft manuscript for editing. This little trick can end up saving you weeks on your overall publishing schedule. It works like this: you submit your draft manuscript to both your editor and designer. While your editor is finessing the manuscript, your designer can be working on developing the overall look and feel for your book's artwork and can be working out the page layout, chapter, heading and copy formatting, image treatments and so on, using the draft copy.

They can also be making a start on the cover design which, when finished, will allow you to start actively promoting your book and building interest prior to its release. Then when the editor has finished their work and the manuscript is finalised, your designer can jump straight into final typesetting, because all the preliminary design decisions have already been made and set into a master template.

Print specifications

In addition to making your book look great, a good designer can also help to make sure that you earn a good return on your investment. Here's how.

The technical specifications of your book directly determine how expensive it will be to print and ship, which in turn directly impacts how much profit, or royalty, you will make from each copy sold. A good book designer can be an invaluable resource in helping you to decide on what format your book should take to optimise your level of royalty, while still being suitable for your market and audience. For example, should your book be hardcover or paperback? What size should it be? Should it have a full-colour interior or just black & white? Even down to helping to decide what grade of paper stock and print quality you will need.

If your designer is really good and has experience in publishing management, they can take all of these criteria, benchmark them against market research of similar books in your genre, and factor in optimal wholesale discounts to help you to determine your final cover price. Once you have that worked out, it is a basic equation to calculate your estimated royalty. See more on royalty calculations in the Pricing section on page 66.

The book design process

I know I've touched on a number of the book design steps, but I think it is essential to briefly run through the basic process your designer will go through to design your book. Designers will each work slightly differently, but at least after this, you will be able to hold an informed discussion with him or her about their workflow.

1. **Design brief/consultation.** Generally conducted very early on in the discussions about your book and ideally before you have committed to a

chosen designer. This step is intended for you to tell the designer about your ideas, preferred style, and provide them with guidance on what you like and don't like. It is beneficial to give examples of books that you admire and are relevant, but make sure your designer doesn't just copy them.

2. **Concept development.** Ideally, you will have chosen a designer who doesn't work from pre-generated templates, so their first job is to come up with some concept layouts, usually based on a couple of pages from your book. These should incorporate the requirements discussed during the consultation. These concepts should give an indication as to page layout, text formatting, image treatment (if required), information hierarchy, and colour palette (if applicable). The designer will send you various options for you to consider and choose from. Depending on the terms of your contract with them, you may have the opportunity to request revisions prior to making a final decision.

3. **Template generation.** Next, your designer will take your chosen concept and expand it into a master template where every aspect that will be required to create your completed book will be standardised. Master pages will be created for all your chapters and/or various page types; style sheets will be generated for every heading level and type of text that your book contains (i.e. quotes, callouts, bullet points, image captions, etc.), as well as the formatting for any tables that your book may have. All these things ensure consistency throughout your book.

4. **Typesetting.** Now that all the design decisions have been made, your designer can proceed with typesetting your book from start to finish, including the placement of any images, charts or graphs that your book contains. Next, the designer will add in any table of contents, index, and references that may be required. Once the initial typesetting is done, a good designer will go back through the book and fine-tune the formatting to eliminate any widows and orphans and fix any awkward line and page breaks before sending you a PDF proof.

5. **Proofing.** The terms of your contract with your designer will determine how many rounds of proofs you get to review before signing off your book, but you want to make sure that there is at least one. During this stage, the onus is fully on you to review the proofs provided by your designer as carefully as possible. Even though a professional will likely have edited your book by this stage, still take the time to read it through line by line again – you'd be surprised at what you can spot now that your book is in a different format. Each designer will have a preference as to how they want to receive amendments back, but the best way is to make notes directly in the PDF using the Comments tools that are available in Adobe Reader or Acrobat Pro. If you're not sure how to use these tools, ask your designer.

6. **Cover Design.** Some designers will prefer to do the cover design first; others will save it for last. Neither way is right or wrong, although my preference is for doing it first (or at least in conjunction with the interior concept development phase), so that you have it fairly early on in the process to use in pre-launch marketing activities. The process for designing your cover is pretty much the same as for the interior. Your designer will present a number of concepts for your consideration, and after some back and forth with suggestions and revisions, you'll end up with a final front cover that your designer will expand on to generate the back cover and spine art.

7. **Final Export.** Once all designs are finalised and you are satisfied with the results, it's time for your designer to export the approved artwork into press-ready PDF files that comply with the technical specifications of your book and the requirements of your printer or publisher.

eBook conversion

Not all books are suitable for the eBook format (such as image intensive art books), but you should always consider having an eBook edition of your book available, as it increases your potential book sales.

There are a few different types of eBooks which you should be familiar with before you start any eBook conversion process, as there are some considerable differences.

The first is an interactive PDF. This is a PDF document where any references, links, table of contents and indexes have been converted into active hyperlinks which the reader can click. For example, if you are reading the eBook version of this book, then you can click on this link right now: www.swatt-books.co.uk. The layout & formatting will appear identical to the print version of the book, and the reader is unable to alter the sizing of the text or images in any way other than being able to zoom into the page as a whole.

Though not technically an eBook format, interactive PDFs have started to get lumped into the eBook pot due to the prevalence of free lead-magnet style eBooks being delivered in PDF format. These types of eBooks are the easiest to create from the print artwork you already have, and most designers will usually include the option free of charge. Note however that PDF eBooks are not compatible with eBook retail sites such as the Kindle, Nook and iBooks stores, though most of these devices are able to read PDF format files if manually loaded onto the device.

The second and most common format is Reflowable ePub. This format is basically a hybrid between your original manuscript and a website. It uses a slightly condensed version of HTML and CSS as its coding language to determine how the formatting appears. A good eBook designer will be able to replicate the design style of your print book fairly closely. However, be aware that, as with a website, the final appearance is governed by the settings on the reading device. This means that the reader can alter the font and text size to suit them, making your book potentially look quite different from what you intended.

Another aspect to note about reflowable ePub format is that due to the reader being able to alter the size of text, page numbers are no longer relevant; hence the "reflowable" part of the name. Text can be split into chapters and sections, but within a chapter or section, the text is one continuous page. This is important to note if your book contains any cross referencing.

The third eBook format is Fixed Format ePub, which is basically a hybrid between PDF and reflowable ePub. Pages are fixed to look exactly as they do in the print artwork but are generated using ePub coding, making them compatible with most later generation eReaders.

This particular format is not very popular due to its lack of support from older devices and its fixed layout nature which makes it difficult to read on smaller screens. I would only recommend using this format if the overall layout of each page is somehow vital to the usability or readability of the book.

The final eBook format is MOBI. This format is almost identical to reflowable ePub, but it is proprietary to Amazon and is for use on Kindle only. When you submit an ePub to Amazon for listing on the Kindle store, it is converted to MOBI format. Due to its proprietary nature, MOBI format is not readable by non-Amazon eBook readers such as Nook or Kobo.

eBook conversion vs generation

Now that you understand the different eBook formats, how do you go about creating one? The answer is you convert it from what you have already.

If you are only wanting to publish your book as an eBook, you would convert it from your Word manuscript once you have finished writing and editing. However, most authors will want to publish their book in both print and eBook formats, in which case you convert the eBook from the completed print-ready artwork to ensure as much similarity between print and eBook editions as possible.

In either instance, be aware that just exporting the artwork or manuscript to ePub format is not the end of the story. Though programs like Word and InDesign are capable of exporting directly to the ePub format, the resulting code that is generated can be very clunky and can result in parts of your book not rendering properly or even not at all, causing errors. To generate a good quality eBook, you will need to open your exported ePub in an eBook editor such as Calibre or Scribe. These programs will allow you to edit and tidy up the code generated by Word or InDesign to make it cleaner and more efficient. I would, however, advise that you have a basic understanding of HTML and CSS style sheets before attempting this yourself, as without the proper knowledge you can break more than you fix.

This is where your designer comes back into play. If you chose a good designer to create your print artwork, they should also be able to do the conversion and tidying up of your eBook for you. They should also perform all the necessary testing to make sure your eBook works on different eReaders such as Kindle, Nook, Kobo and iBooks, as well as smartphones and tablets. If they aren't able to do this as part of the design process, then you may need to find an eBook specialist to do the conversion for you. Personally, I would make eBook conversion knowledge part of the selection criteria when looking to hire your book designer, as it will save you money in the long run.

How you can help

As with any client/supplier relationship, the more you can support the supplier, the easier and often cheaper the experience will be. So how can you the author help your designer?

First off, be clear about what you want to see during the brief. If there are things you like or don't like, things that must be incorporated (such as branding guidelines) or limiting factors about your readers (such as they're older and may have trouble reading small print), tell your designer about them right from the very start. That way the designer can work them into the initial concept development, instead of trying to shoehorn them in later.

Secondly, be open-minded. Even if you have a firm idea of how you want your book to look, be open-minded to suggestions your designer makes even if they don't necessarily fit with the vision you have in your head. After all, they are the professionals and they will have reasons behind their suggestions. Consider these suggestions from the point of view of your reader and be rational.

Next, once your designer has started typesetting, it is important that you stop writing! This doesn't mean that you cannot change anything, but you need to remember that once typesetting starts, your book should no longer be in Word format; any changes you make to the Word manuscript will not be reflected in the typeset artwork. So, wait until the proofing stage to make amendments.

Try to confirm as much of the design during the concept development stage as possible. Making changes to the overall design and formatting of the book can be much more challenging and time-consuming once the book has been fully typeset. So, when reviewing concept designs, be sure to consider them against how that concept will work when applied to the entire book. Also, make a point to print out a couple of pages from each concept at 100% scale (not fit to page) so that you can accurately get a feel for text size and readability.

Lastly, understand the contract you have with your designer in terms of what is included and what is not, especially when it comes to how many rounds of revisions have been allowed for, and if there are any restrictions as to what type of revisions are permitted within the fees agreed. That way there are no surprises or uncomfortable conversations later on about invoice charges.

Images

There is another important area in which you can help to support your designer which warrants its own section, and that is the supply of images.

If your book is going to contain images, charts or graphs, there are various considerations that you need to take into account to make sure that they are suitable for use within your book and to reduce the amount of work that your designer will need to do to accommodate those images.

Resolution

Image resolution is something that most people outside of the design industry don't know much about. However, it can have a profound effect on the quality of your published book. All professional printing requires images to be a minimum of 300dpi in resolution (which means that every square inch is made up of a minimum of 300 pixels). Images that are used for screen purposes, such as on websites, are only 72dpi, so just copying an image from your website (or worse still, someone else's website) is not good enough. Always try to send your designer the highest resolution images you have available. If you're not sure, send them the images with the largest file size and ask them to check if they are sufficient.

Colour mode

This is another legacy of the differences between screen and print use. Printers print in CMYK, which means that every colour you see printed is made up of a combination of Cyan, Magenta, Yellow and Black (or Key) inks. Images on screen are made up of RGB, a combination of Red, Green and Blue pixels. RGB images change colour slightly when printed because there is not an exact conversion from RGB to CMYK. To make sure that the colours within your book are going to reproduce accurately, be sure to supply images that are in CMYK colour mode. The downside to this is that most people don't have access to software that is able to do this conversion accurately. If you are unsure, inform your designer early on that you will be supplying images, but that you are unable to confirm what colour mode they will be in. They can then include the time in their quotation to check and, if necessary, convert those images.

Copyright

This is not so much a design issue as a legal and ethical one. If you are going to use images in your book, be sure that you have the rights to use them. To be 100% certain on that either create your own (or ask your designer to create them) or purchase suitable images from a reputable stock image library.

The reason why I mention it here is that while your designer would be the first port of call in the event of any copyright breach, if they can prove that you supplied the images, then you will be liable not them.

File format

The final consideration is the file format that you supply your images in. Some file formats are better quality than others. For example, Tiff is better quality than JPEG and EPS is better for print than PNG. Ask your designer what file format they would prefer images to be delivered in and be honest if you are unable to supply the formats that they request. There is a good chance that they will still be able to use them, but they will need to factor in a bit of time for conversion.

This is particularly important when it comes to the supply of charts and graphs. In an ideal world, charts and graphs should be formatted in the same style as the typesetting of the book itself. In order to do this, most charts and graphs will need to be recreated. If you can supply the source data for these graphics, then it will make the designer's job much easier – possibly even eliminating the need to recreate the images at all.

Chapter 5

Publishing

So, all your hard work has paid off; you now have a well-written book that looks great and is ready to be released to the world. Now it's time to actually "publish".

Publishing Methods

As we touched on in Chapter Two, you have a number of options of how you publish your book; eBook only, Print on Demand, or self-fulfilment. Each option has its pros and cons depending on the type of book you are releasing, but the most popular approach is a combination of all three. Here's how each method works:

eBook only

You publish your book as a digital eBook onto the Kindle store (Amazon) as well as Kobo (Rakuten), Nook (Barnes & Noble), and iBook stores (Apple). This gives your book distribution throughout Europe, North America and Australia on the four most popular e-reading devices. As there are no production costs, you will retain a higher percentage of the cover price as a royalty. However, as it is a digital format, readers are accustomed to paying a much lower purchase price.

Offering an eBook in conjunction with a print edition gives you two bites of the cherry, as many avid readers will buy a hard copy for their library but will also purchase an eBook edition to read while on holiday or during their daily commute.

Print on Demand

Print on Demand (or PoD for short) technology has revolutionised the publishing industry in recent decades. It allows for micro print runs of a book at a similar quality to traditional printers. The premise is that if you group together different books with the same print specifications (colour, paper stock, and trim size), it doesn't matter how many copies of each book are printed, as the number of different books together will make up the full print run. This premise makes it possible to print as few as a single copy of a book including binding. PoD books are printed digitally as opposed to litho. However, modern digital printing presses are getting better and better, and unless your book includes very detailed high definition photographs requiring a print resolution of higher than 300dpi, the average reader would be unable to distinguish the difference. The one drawback of PoD printing is the requirement for your book to comply with specific print specifications. This means that unusual trim sizes or special print finishes such as foil blocking or spot UV are not allowed.

The distribution of PoD books is taken care of by the book supplier. In the case of Ingram Spark (the largest PoD self-publishing platform currently available), they have access to a distribution network of over 7,000 online book retailers, libraries and universities worldwide. The process basically works like this: a customer places an order for your book with an online retailer, let's use Waterstones as an example. Waterstones' system informs Ingram Spark about the order specifics, including which book was ordered and the customer's delivery address. Ingram Spark prints one copy of your book and ships it directly to the customer – usually in the branded packaging of the retailer (if it's a large company). The cost of printing is deducted from the wholesale price that the retailers pay (which is a fixed amount), and whatever is left over makes up your royalty. There is no need for you to get involved in the process at all, except to be notified at the end of the month how many books have been sold during that billing cycle.

Self-distribution

With self-distribution publishing you have the greatest control, but it also requires the highest amount of investment and involvement on your part. In this publishing model, you source a traditional printer to print a run of your book as a single consignment. Because your book is the only one on the press at any one time, there are no limitations on your print specifications outside of what your budget can afford. What you do need to bear in mind is that there will be a minimum print quantity required by the printer, usually around 500 copies. Though you can sometimes negotiate down to 250, your cost per copy will inevitably rise. You will also need to have a secure, dry, dark location in which to store your books once they are printed and delivered to you; preferably somewhere that has forklift/pallet truck facilities, because 500+ books will most likely arrive on a pallet. It is then up to you to arrange distribution agreements with individual retailers or hire a wholesale distributor such as Gardners or Bertrams to manage the distribution of your book into retail bookstores.

To get your book listed on Amazon is fairly straightforward; you just need to sign up for a Distributed by Amazon account. You will then be required to send a shipment of books to an Amazon central warehouse, from which Amazon will then manage the shipping to its customers.

This publishing model is by far the most complex and requires you to have a good head for sales, finance and negotiation. However, it can give you the largest long-term financial reward if you work at it.

Recommended Combination Model

The publishing model that I would recommend for 90% of self-published books is a combination approach (also known as a dual publishing model) that incorporates a combination of all three options. In a dual publishing approach, you create eBook and PoD accounts with both Amazon KDP and Ingram Spark. The account with KDP fulfils all retail sales of both Kindle and print editions of your book through Amazon. Your Ingram Spark account gives your book further worldwide distribution to retail channels outside of Amazon such as Waterstones, Barnes & Noble, Chapters/Indigo, The Book Depository plus 7k other online book retailers and libraries for both your print and eBook editions.

You then use the PoD print facilities of your Ingram Spark account to order your own stock of books for selling yourself or for marketing purposes. If you suddenly find yourself requiring a large number of books at any one time (more than 300 copies) then you would find a traditional printer to produce a one-off print run using the same specifications as your PoD copies. This option gives you the widest possible distribution with the least amount of investment or setup of infrastructure.

The How To guides throughout the rest of this book will walk you through the exact step-by-step process for following this publishing model.

Pricing

Now that you have considered how you are going to get your book to market, it's time to start working out your pricing. This is a bit different to the budgeting exercise we did in Chapter Two, as instead of looking at how much it is going to cost you to get your book published, we are going to work out how much you should sell your book for.

Firstly, you need to research what other books similar to yours are retailing for. Look for books in the same genre that have similar subject matter and length. Take an average of their cover prices and use that as a starting point to set a target cover price for your book. Don't forget to factor in your reputation and experience if you are writing non-fiction, as your knowledge has value.

When you have a target cover price in mind, subtract from that the wholesale discount. This is the price that a retailer will buy your book for and determines how much profit they make from selling a copy of your book. Some retailers will have a set discount that they demand, with others it is negotiable. The average can vary quite widely, from 35% all the way up to 55%. Obviously, the higher the wholesale discount, the more attractive your book is to the retailer, but the lower your profit. I usually start with a discount of 45%.

Next, you need to subtract your per unit production costs. This is how much it costs you to print each copy. For the self-distribution model, this is the cost of your print run (including delivery both to you and to your reader) divided by the number of copies printed. For PoD books, this is the production cost of each copy based on the print specification of the book as set by the publishing platform.

The amount that is left over is your profit, or royalty. If this figure is not entirely to your liking, or worse still is negative, then you can go back and alter either the starting cover price or the wholesale discount you are offering until this balances out. This can take quite a bit of trial and error to get right. If you are using Ingram Spark as your PoD platform, they have a very helpful set of calculators on their website for both print production costs and publisher compensation that makes working out this balance much easier: https://myaccount.ingramspark. com/Portal/Tools/PubCompCalculator.

Here's a sample calculation so that you can see the numbers in action. Let's assume your book has the following specifications:

Trim size: 5.5 x 8.5
Printing: Full colour on 70lb white paper stock
Binding: Perfect bound paperback with matte cover
Page count: 200 pp

The calculation would look a bit like this:

Target cover price – wholesale discount – print charge = royalty
£14.99 – 45% – £4.80 = £3.44

A common mistake that many authors make is trying to include their initial investment of editing and design into their cover price calculation. This can lead to figures just not adding up unless you set a ridiculously high cover price, which could price your book out of the market. If you are concerned about being able to recuperate your initial book creation expenses, create a separate calculation that looks at how many books you need to sell at the royalty amount you determined in the previous exercise in order to break even. This will give you a more realistic view of when your book will become profitable without over-inflating your cover price and thus impacting sales.

Metadata

The last portion of preparation work that you need to do before listing your book is to finalise your metadata. Metadata is like SEO for books; it is how people find out about your book online who don't yet know that your book exists.

There are three main components that make up your book's metadata: Description, Keywords, and Categorisation.

Description

Most authors assume that the description of their book, also referred to as a synopsis, is what is written on the back cover. In most instances that is true; however, Ingram Spark splits this into two parts – a short and a long description. The long description IS generally the text from your back cover, but the short description is limited to 350 characters (including spaces and punctuation) and is a mandatory field. This means you need to give your synopsis a bit more thought. I find the best way to think of a synopsis is to treat it like an elevator pitch. In the span of 60 seconds or less, explain what your book is about and who it will benefit. For example, here is the synopsis for this book:

> *Stress-Free Self-Publishing gives independent authors a no-nonsense guide to taking control of self-publishing in a way that is professional, credible and ethical. Using proven methods, our approach ensures that authors retain 100% of their copyright and royalties and opens up affordable distribution into 7000+ online retailers worldwide.*

Keywords

Keywords for your book are no different than the keywords you use to optimise your website. They are the words and phrases that ordinary people would use to search for a book with your book's subject matter. For example, here are some of the keywords I have used for this book:

- Self-publishing
- Publishing a book
- IngramSpark
- KDP publishing
- Publish your own book
- Print on demand books
- Amazon self-publishing

- Online book publishing
- Independent publishing
- Direct publishing
- Cost to self-publish a book
- How to publish your book
- Best way to publish a book
- How to self-publish

If you're not familiar with SEO and keywords, a good resource to look at is the Google Keyword Planner (https://ads.google.com/aw/keywordplanner). This service is intended for finding optimised keywords for websites, but it is equally useful for your book. Simply start with the primary keyword that you believe relates to your book and the tool will give you a list of suggestions based on the search history of Google users. Keep feeding keyword ideas in and then develop a comprehensive list. Note that you will need a Google account in order to access this service.

Categorisation

The final, and most important, part of your metadata are the categories in which your book is listed in online stores. It is critical that you choose the correct category for your book in Amazon, Ingram Spark and others, as this is often the start-point for people's search online. Think of the category as your book's genre but then refined into one or more sub-genres. The more focused and clearly defined you can get the better. For example, if I had just finished reading the *Game of Thrones* series and was looking for a novel on Amazon which was similar, I could drill right down through a series of genres and sub-genres. My category search journey could be: Books > Science Fiction & Fantasy > Fantasy > Sword & Sorcery and then even a filter in the Fantasy Characters sidebar menu, ticking

'Dragons'. I am now looking at a manageable list of relevant books to choose from. This is the goal for your book.

So, there are two main reasons why you need to put a lot of thought into this as a self-published author. The first is your competition. When someone is just browsing through Amazon and not looking for a specific book, they will generally start by selecting the category that interests them. The fewer titles there are in that category, the more likely that they will find your book. Secondly, Amazon sales rankings are based on sales figures compared against other titles in your category. So, the more specific you are about your category(s) the better your chances of performing well in that category. The classic route to claiming 'bestseller' status on Amazon is to achieve this in a tightly-defined category with a surprisingly small level of sale.

It is worth noting that Ingram Spark and Amazon use different categorising systems, so it is important that you research both. Ingram Spark uses the BASIC Subject Heading system, find out more at https://bisg.org/page/bisacedition.

Amazon have their own systems for print and Kindle separately, so the best approach is to look through the Amazon categories as if you were a consumer. Go onto the Books section of the Amazon site and you will see 'Advanced Search' in the menu bar. In here you can search by entering various criteria, from specific titles and ISBN numbers down to more general filters such as 'Keywords' and 'Subject': 'Subject' is the word used by Amazon in this context for category. Look at the subject drop-down choices, think about the keyword search for your own book and enter these into these two respective fields and see what comes up. If books which you consider to be your closest competitors appear, then you know your own choice of keywords and category are along the right lines.

Now that you know which publishing route you are going to use, have calculated your pricing and finalised your metadata, it is time to finally get down to brass tacks and publish your book. The next chapter is an illustrated How To guide that will walk you through each of the steps required for getting yourself registered as a self-publisher and listing your book.

Chapter 6

The Step by Step Guide

PHASE 1: Registering as a self-publisher

The first step in the actual process of publishing your book is to register yourself as a self-publisher with the ISBN agency for your region. In the UK and Ireland that agency is Nielsen's, and in the US and Australia, it's Bowker. A list of other ISBN agencies is listed at the back of this book. Registration is a very straightforward process and consists of supplying your publisher details: imprint name, registered address, contact telephone number and email address.

You should note that these details will become public record, so if you have concerns regarding your privacy you can submit your address as a PO box and set up a separate email address for your publishing activities. I would recommend doing this anyway as it makes you look more professional. Your imprint name is basically the company name you will publish under. This can be your real or pen name, or you can make up a company name that suits you. Your publishing imprint does not need to be an official company that is registered with the government; however, if you hope to make a lot of money from your book(s) or plan on publishing a number of books under the same imprint you might want to consider registering your imprint as a company for tax purposes. If you're unsure whether you should do this or not, speak to an accountant or tax advisor.

How To: Set up a self-publishing account with Nielsen's

Registration process

Go to https://www.nielsenisbnstore.com/Account/Register and this is the page that you will see.

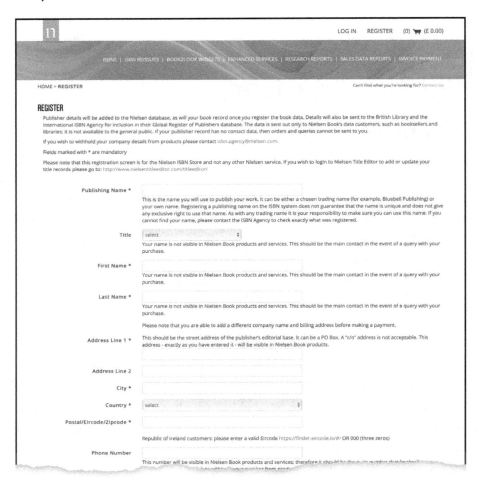

Phone Number	This number will be visible in Nielsen Book products and services; therefore it should be the main number that booksellers can contact you on. If you wish to withhold your number from products and services please contact isbn.agency@nielsen.com.
Fax Number	This number will be visible in Nielsen Book products and services; therefore it should be the main number that booksellers can contact you on. If you wish to withhold your number from products and services please contact isbn.agency@nielsen.com.
Website	This site will be visible in Nielsen Book products and services. If you wish to withhold your website from products and services please contact isbn.agency@nielsen.com. If ebooks are available as downloads from your own website, you must enter the website here.
VAT Number	Only required if you are VAT registered in Ireland
Organisation Type *	select
Company Structure *	select
What type of material do you publish? *	select
	○ Please tick if you are a new publisher or self-published author.
Print Distributor *	Please tell us the distributor of your printed material. If you self-distribute, please indicate that here. If you use a third party, you must give us their name and address.
eBook Distributor *	Please tell us the distributor of your ebooks. If you self-distribute, please indicate that here. If you use a third party, you must give us their name and address.
	○ Please tick if you are a new publisher or self-published author.
Email *	
Confirm Email *	

- The email you provide will be your username for the ISBN Store.
- The email will be visible in Nielsen Book products and services; therefore it should be an email that you are happy for booksellers to contact you on. If you wish to withhold your email from products and services please contact isbn.agency@nielsen.com.
- The email you provide will be used to send confirmation of any purchases you make through the ISBN Store.
- If you have indicated that you will self-distribute print books, we will set you up to receive your orders electronically using this email. If you wish to amend this later, please contact supplydata.book@nielsen.com.

Password Rules	Please note that your password must have:
	  • At least 6 characters
	  • At least 1 uppercase character (A-Z)
	  • At least 1 lowercase character (a-z)
	  • At least 1 number (0-9)
	  • At least 1 special character (!@#$%^&*()-_=+~)

Password *	
Confirm password *	
Marketing Opt In	○ Please tick the box for your company/organisation to receive marketing information from Nielsen Book Services Ltd in the future. We maintain customer records for all our clients (paying and non-paying) and use this information to communicate either by post, telephone or email, to ensure that you are kept up-to-date with information about the Nielsen Book services you use. We try to keep these messages relevant and to a minimum. We also keep our clients fully informed of our latest news, forthcoming events and relevant industry updates via our marketing communications, by email and post. NB: We will however continue to communicate with you as a client by keeping you fully informed of any relevant service information. These will cover any changes to our services (both free and subscription based) and where necessary important information about your title records and government legislation that may have an impact on the service we provide to you. **Note: Please verify your address details, if you are not happy with your details, complete registration and contact us at isbn.agency@nielsen.com. Please do NOT purchase any products until address details are corrected.**
Terms of Service	○ Accept the Terms of Service for the ISBN Store

REGISTER >   **CANCEL**

nielsen

COMPANY INFO
About Us
Contact Us

FAQS
New Publishers
Existing Publishers

Secured by sage Pay VISA

Privacy & Cookie Policy | Terms of Use
Copyright © 2019 Nielsen BookServices Ltd. All Rights Reserved.
Powered by SAPnet

Nielsen is very good at explaining each section of the form and what information is required, but I'll run through it all for you here just in case.

1. **Publishing Name** – this will become your imprint name. As mentioned before this can be your real name, a pen name, or a company name that you either trade under already or create for the purpose of publishing your books.

2. **Title** – this is your title (Ms, Mrs, Mr, Dr, etc.)

3. **First Name / Last Name** – these are required fields but are not made visible to the public through any of Nielsen's services.

4. **Address** – this is basically the trading address of your publishing imprint. It can be a PO box but cannot be a forwarding address or c/o address. Note that this address WILL be visible in all of Nielsen's services.

5. **Phone Number / Fax Number / Website** – these contact details are not required fields; however I do recommend that you fill in at least one of them so that retailers using any of the Nielsen Book services to order books will be able to get in touch with you should they have any questions or need to order books from you directly (in the case of self-fulfilment publishing).

6. **VAT Number** – this is only required if you are VAT registered in Ireland. Reason for this is publishers located in the Republic of Ireland or the Channel Islands are not charged VAT on ISBN numbers.

7. **Organisation Type** – this is basically who you are in the publishing food-chain. If you are reading this book, then choose "Self-Publisher".

8. **Company Structure** – this is how your publishing imprint is set up. If you are just publishing under your own name then select "Sole Trader"; if you are publishing through a company or other such organisation, then chose one of the other options which best suits the structure of your organisation.

9. **What type of material do you publish?** – is your book(s) going to be an eBook, print book, or both? If you are still not sure at this point, I would select both to cover all your bases.

10. **Please tick if you are a new publisher or self-published author** – this only applies if this is your very first book and you have never published before, even under a different imprint.

11. **Email** – enter your email address and then confirm it. Note that this email address will be visible in Nielsen services, as well as acting as your login ID to access your publishing account in the future. It will also be the email address that Nielsen will use to contact you for any reason regarding your books and account, so make sure that it is an account that you actively monitor.

12. **Password** – choose a password that complies with the stipulations from Nielsen, but also one that you can remember.

Select whether you want to receive marketing information from Nielsen Book Services and tick to accept the Terms of Service for the ISBN Store, and you're done. On clicking REGISTER you will be taken to the ISBN Store where you can purchase your ISBN numbers.

PHASE 2: ISBN numbers

Once you have registered as a self-publisher you are then eligible to purchase ISBN numbers. At the time of publication of this book, you can purchase ISBNs singly or in batches of 10, 50, 100, or 1000 from both Nielsen's and from Bowker. If you are publishing an eBook, it is not a requirement to have an ISBN number assigned to it, but I would strongly recommend that you do, as it makes your eBook more searchable and strengthens your legal rights over it.

So, with that in mind, I always advise my clients to purchase a set of 10 ISBNs to start off with; it gives you the two numbers you need for your current book plus 8 spares that you can use for additional books or second editions. It is useful to remember that ISBN numbers do not expire - however, please note that they are non-transferable.

After you have been assigned your ISBN numbers, you will need to update your print edition artwork to include a scannable ISBN barcode on the back cover and on a verso (or copyright) page at the beginning of the main content of your book. This traditionally falls immediately after the title page. The verso page outlines the legal copyright information for the book, including publication date, ISBN number, publisher details and any other copyright protections you wish to include. Many authors will also include details of who printed the book as well as the designer, illustrator, editor and cover art credits. Note that it is not only good practice to include a verso page in your book for your own legal protection, but it is also a requirement that your ISBN number and the publisher details listed here match those on record with the ISBN agency.

How To: Purchase your ISBN numbers

The screen below is what you will see as soon as you click REGISTER after you have finished registering as a self-publisher with Nielsen's. If for some reason you are coming back to this at a later time, go to https://www.nielsenisbnstore.com/Home/Isbn, login into your self-publishing account using the LOGIN link at the top of the page, and then continue as outlined below.

Step 1:

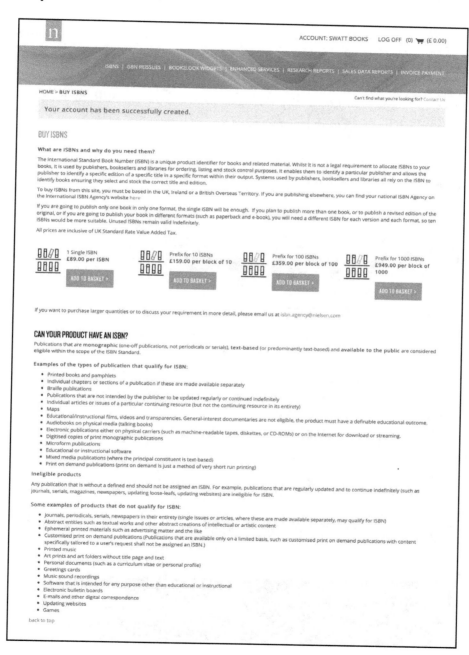

You have 4 options, depending on how many ISBN numbers you wish to purchase. If you are certain that you are only ever going to publish one book and only in one format, then by all means purchase just a single ISBN number. However, it is far more cost effective and future-proof to buy ISBN numbers in batches of 10. That way you have the ability to publish both print and eBook editions of your current book and have 8 ISBN numbers left over should you decide to ever release a 2nd edition or go on to write more books once you've developed a taste for it.

Once you've decided how many ISBNs to purchase, select **ADD TO BASKET**, and you will be taken to the next screen.

Step 2:

Before you proceed any further, you need to make sure that your billing address has been added to your account details.

Click on your Account Name at the top of the page.

Step 3:

Fill in your billing address details and click the checkbox at the top telling Nielsen to use this address for payments. Click **SAVE** , and then click on the shopping trolley icon at the top right corner of the page to go back to the previous page.

Step 4:

Now simply confirm that you are happy with the order. If you have a promotional code, enter it now using the link above and to the right of the Basket Total.

Once you are ready to proceed to pay for your ISBN numbers, tick to accept the Terms & Conditions for ISBN Registration and then click **PROCEED**. You will then be taken to a secure SagePay screen.

Step 5:

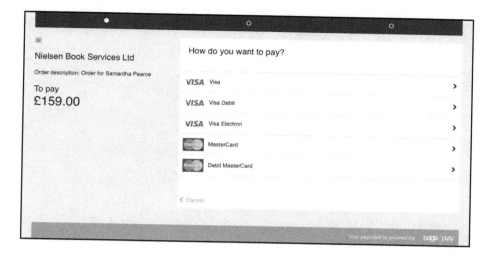

The first Sage Pay screen will ask you to confirm what type of debit/credit card you wish to use.

Step 6:

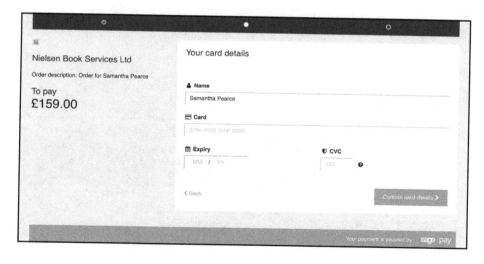

Then you will be asked to fill in the details for your chosen card.

Step 7:

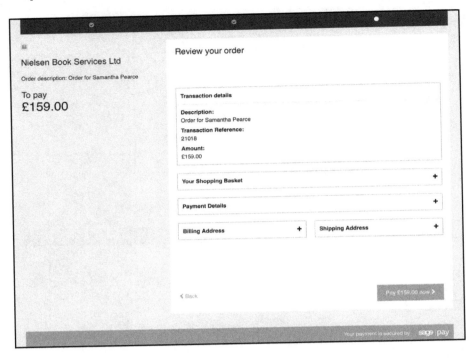

Finally you will be asked to review your order. If you are happy to proceed click **PAY NOW** .

Step 8:

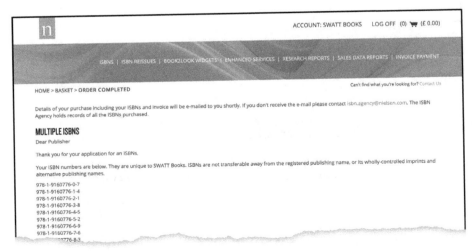

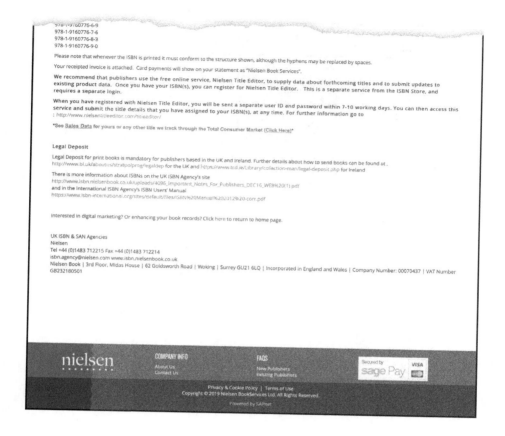

Once your payment has been fully processed, you will arrive at the order confirmation screen where you will see a list of your allocated ISBN numbers. I highly recommend that you save your ISBN numbers into an Excel spreadsheet where you can keep track of what titles you have assigned to which ISBN number, what format of book that ISBN number has been used for, and whether or not that title has been submitted to the Nielsen Book Database (more on that later in this chapter). Here's an example of an ISBN number spreadsheet that I use for my clients.

	A	B	C	D	E	F
1	**SWATT Books Ltd. ISBN #'s**					
2						
3	ISBN #	Title	Format	Database Listing		
4	978-1-9160776-0-7	Stress-Free Self-Publishing	Paperback			
5	978-1-9160776-1-4	Stress-Free Self-Publishing	eBook			
6	978-1-9160776-2-1					
7	978-1-9160776-3-8					
8	978-1-9160776-4-5					
9	978-1-9160776-5-2					
10	978-1-9160776-6-9					
11	978-1-9160776-7-6					
12	978-1-9160776-8-3					
13	978-1-9160776-9-0					
14						
15						
16						

PHASE 3: Setting up your publishing accounts

Now we get to the meat of the process - listing your book. This section assumes that you are following the dual publishing model outlined earlier of releasing both eBook and print editions of your book through Amazon and Ingram Spark.

If this is your first book, then your first task is to set up self-publishing accounts with Amazon KDP and Ingram Spark. Both accounts are free to open, and you will require all the same information you used to register for your ISBN numbers, plus bank account details of where you want your royalties deposited, as well as a debit or credit card to cover any listing and printing fees. Both accounts will require you to complete a tax declaration based on your location as well as agreeing to each platform's terms and conditions of use.

How To: Set up a self-publishing account with Ingram Spark

Go to https://myaccount.ingramspark.com/Account/Signup.

Step 1:

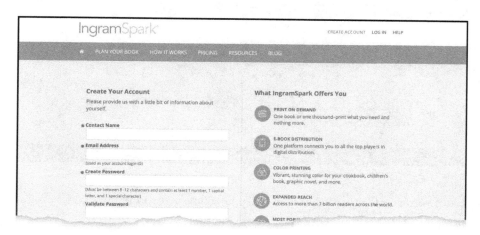

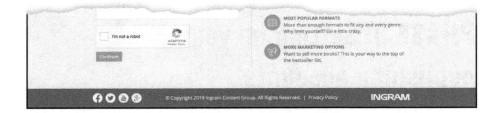

We start off nice and simple: enter your full name, your email address (which will also act as your login ID) and create a password. Check the tick box to bypass the SPAM filter, and then click **CONTINUE**.

Step 2:

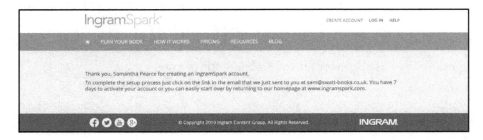

You'll then be presented with this Thank You screen. Shortly afterwards, you will receive an email to the address you provided, with a link to activate the account and confirm your identity.

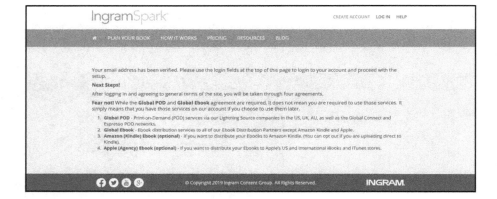

Once you have activated your account, you will be able to sign into your account using the email and password you entered in Step 1.

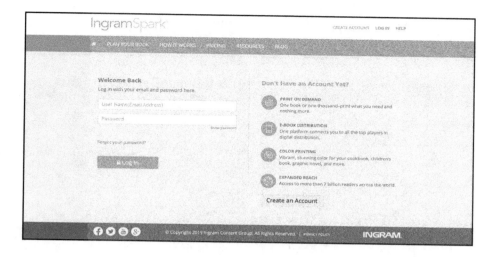

Step 3:

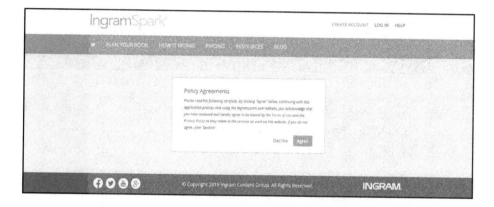

As soon as you log in you will be presented with your Policy Agreements. Read through them carefully and then click **AGREE**.

Step 4:

Next you will be asked to provide your basic business info. This is all the same information that you provided to Nielsen's when you registered for your ISBN account with them, and I would advise that you provide exactly the same data.

The main point of difference is the question, "What Best Describes You?" This is basically finding out where you are on your author journey.

Step 5:

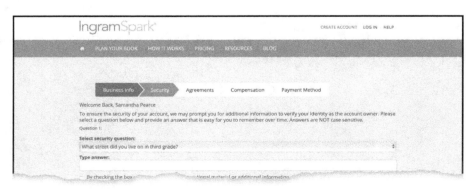

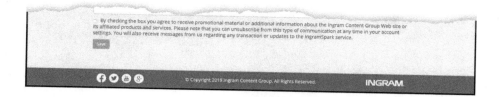

Next, select and then provide the answer to a security question. This will be used should you ever get locked out of your account.

Tick the box at the bottom if you want to receive promotional emails from Ingram Spark and their affiliates. Though I usually always tick that I don't want to receive these sorts of things, in this instance I would highly recommend that you do opt-in; the information that Ingram Spark sends out regularly is very helpful to first-time authors and publishers, and they often run promotional offers for free listings and discounted book printing where promo codes are emailed to account holders in advance.

Click **SAVE** to continue.

Step 6:

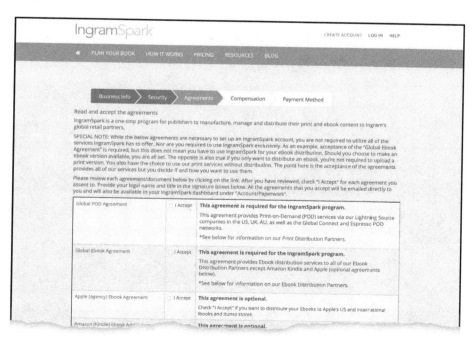

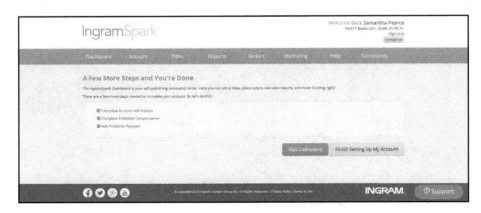

Now we're starting to get to the business end of things. These are your Publishing Agreements. These are very important, as they dictate the terms under which your book will be published with each of Ingram's distribution partners. Take the time to read each agreement thoroughly before ticking to accept each agreement. You will then need to provide an electronic signature at the bottom of the page before you can proceed. By filling in the details at the bottom, you will be legally bound to these publishing agreements for as long as they are in force. Occasionally a distribution partner will update their agreements, in which case Ingram will notify you by email before the new agreement comes into force and you will then be required to sign your acceptance of the new agreement.

Step 7:

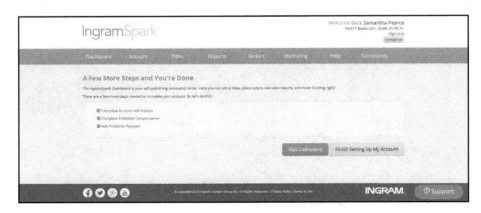

Once you have provided your digital signature accepting your publishing agreements, your account is active enough for you to start having a nose around. However, there are a couple more steps that you need to undertake before you can list your book, so I recommend completing these straightaway. Click on "Finish Setting Up My Account" to continue.

Step 8:

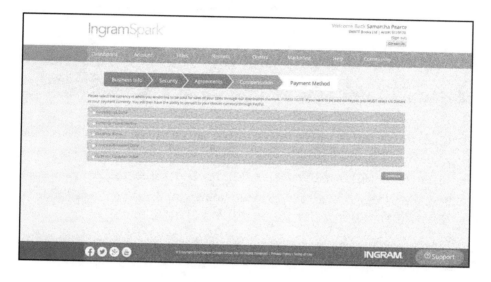

Payment method section: First up is to provide the details for where you would like your Compensation (royalties) to be paid.

Start off by selecting the currency you want to be paid in.

Step 9:

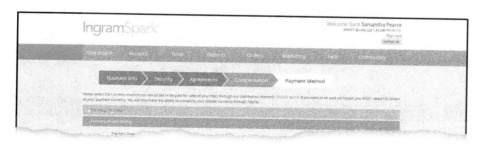

Then fill in the details for the bank account into which your royalties should be paid. If you would like to receive a remittance advice (which is basically a payment confirmation) once each payment has been made, confirm your email address. This does not have to be the same address as the account email address.

Step 10:

The next and final step is to provide a method of payment. Ingram Spark requires you to always have an active, valid debit or credit card on file to cover printing costs and listing fees. You have the option of changing the payment card used during each transaction, but for security, you need to have at least one card permanently saved on file.

To add a card, click on **ADD NEW CARD** .

Step 11:

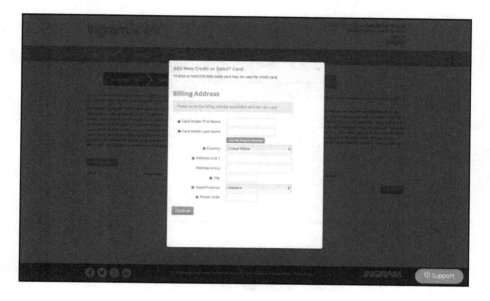

Start off by filling in all your billing details including name and billing address. If you live outside of the United States or Canada, simply select Not Applicable for the State/Province dropdown.

Click **CONTINUE** .

Step 12:

Next, select the type of card you are adding, then provide the long card number from the front and the expiration date.

Then click **FINISH**.

Step 13:

And that's it – your account is set up!

Click **GO TO DASHBOARD** , which will look like this:

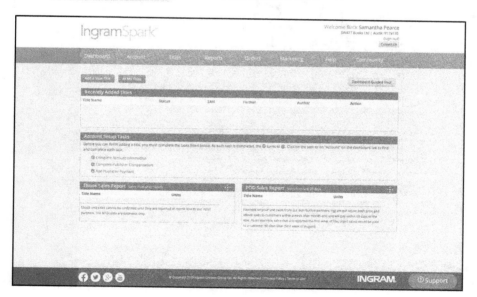

How To: Set up a self-publishing account with KDP (Amazon)

Before we begin, I would recommend that you sign out of any Amazon account(s) you have, so that you don't accidentally link your KDP account to any personal shopping accounts you may have. Once you have done that, start by visiting https://kdp.amazon.com.

Step 1:

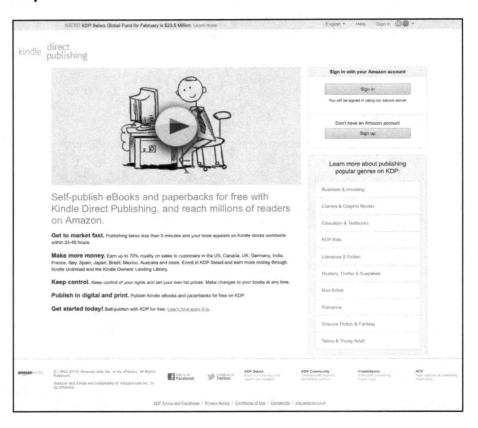

You have two options to proceed from here: you can sign into an existing Amazon account, or you can create an Amazon account from scratch. I would only recommend using an existing Amazon account if you are publishing a book solely under your own name for your own purposes and not in relation to any existing company or organisation, even if that company is wholly owned by you.

If you opt to continue by signing into a pre-existing Amazon account, you will be taken to the KDP login page. Note that you have the option to change your mind and create a new KDP account at the bottom of the page.

Step 2:

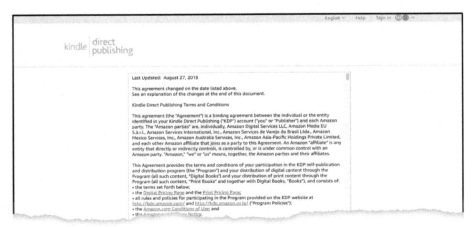

...eating an account, you agree to Amazon's
Conditions of Use and Privacy Notice.

Already have an account? Sign in ›

KDP Terms and Conditions   Conditions of Use   Privacy Notice   Help

© 1996-2019, Amazon.com, Inc. or its affiliates

If you opt to create a new Amazon account (which I recommend), you will be taken to an initial account creation form where you fill in your name, email address, and select a password. Once you click **CREATE YOUR KDP ACCOUNT** Amazon will send you an email to verify your email address.

kindle | direct publishing

Verify email address

To verify your email, we've sent a code to
sam@swatt-books.co.uk (Change)

Enter code

[   ]

[Verify   ]

Resend code

KDP Terms and Conditions   Conditions of Use   Privacy Notice   Help

© 1996-2019, Amazon.com, Inc. or its affiliates

Step 3:

kindle | direct publishing

English ˅   Help   Sign in

Last Updated: August 27, 2018

This agreement changed on the date listed above.
See an explanation of the changes at the end of this document.

Kindle Direct Publishing Terms and Conditions

This agreement (the "Agreement") is a binding agreement between the individual or the entity identified in your Kindle Direct Publishing ("KDP") account ("you" or "Publisher") and each Amazon party. The "Amazon parties" are, individually, Amazon Digital Services LLC, Amazon Media EU S.à.r.l., Amazon Services International, Inc., Amazon Serviços de Varejo do Brasil Ltda., Amazon Mexico Services, Inc., Amazon Australia Services, Inc., Amazon Asia-Pacific Holdings Private Limited, and each other Amazon affiliate that joins as a party to this Agreement. An Amazon "affiliate" is any entity that directly or indirectly controls, is controlled by, or is under common control with an Amazon party. "Amazon," "we" or "us" means, together, the Amazon parties and their affiliates.

This Agreement provides the terms and conditions of your participation in the KDP self-publication and distribution program (the "Program") and your distribution of digital content through the Program (all such content, "Digital Books") and your distribution of print content through the Program (all such content, "Print Books" and together with Digital Books, "Books"), and consists of:
• the terms set forth below;
• the Digital Pricing Page and the Print Pricing Page;
• all rules and policies for participating in the Program provided on the KDP website at http://kdp.amazon.com/ and http://kdp.amazon.co.jp/ ("Program Policies");
• the Amazon.com Conditions of Use; and
• the Amazon... Notice.

Once you have verified your email address, you will be asked to agree to the Kindle Direct Publishing Terms and Conditions. These look very boring, but please do read through these carefully and then click **AGREE** when you are ready to continue.

Step 4:

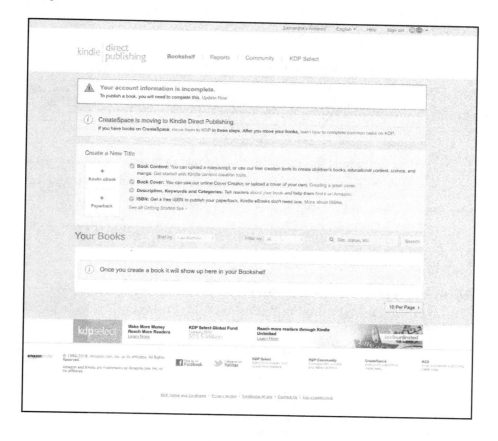

You will now be taken to your KDP Dashboard, where you can start adding titles straightaway. However, you will need to complete your account information before you are able to publish a book, so let's do that right now. Click on **UPDATE NOW** , located in the gold warning box at the top of the screen.

Step 5:

There are three additional sets of details that Amazon requires to complete your account setup – Author/Publisher Information, Payment Details, and your Tax Information. Start off by selecting your country or region of residence.

Step 6:

Once you have selected your country, the box will expand to allow you to enter your full address and contact telephone number. When you have completed that, in the next section, select the location of the bank you wish to use to receive your royalty payments.

Step 7:

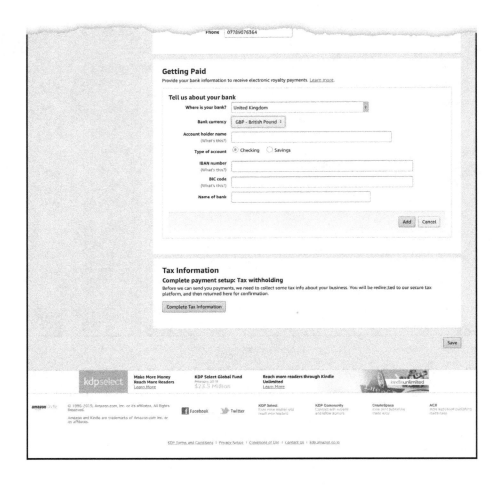

You will now be able to provide the details of the bank account where you require your royalty payments to be deposited. Note that all fields need to be completed.

Once you have entered in all your bank details, click **ADD** and Amazon will do a quick check to verify your account. If that all passes, you will see a check mark appear in the "Getting Paid" section.

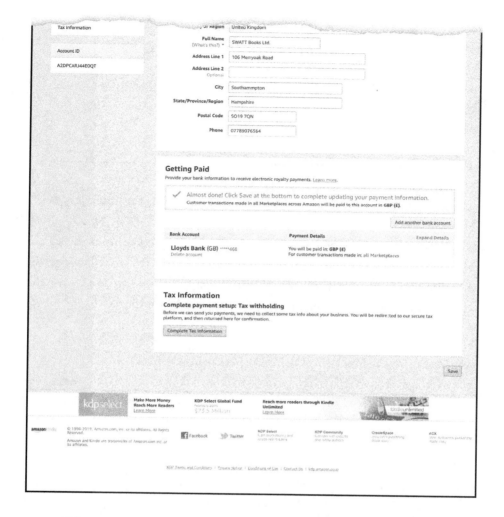

Click **SAVE** at the bottom of the screen and then select **COMPLETE TAX INFORMATION** in the next section.

Step 8:

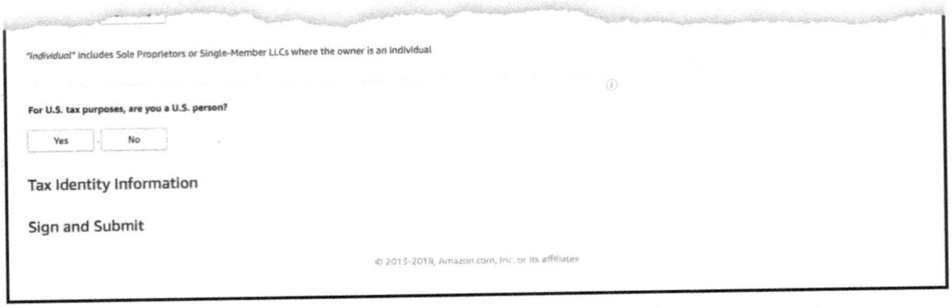

"Individual" includes Sole Proprietors or Single-Member LLCs where the owner is an individual
For U.S. tax purposes, are you a U.S. person?
Yes
No
Tax Identity Information
Sign and Submit
© 2013-2018, Amazon.com, Inc. or its affiliates

You will be taken to a new page to complete a Tax Information Interview.

The first question is simply who will be receiving the income from the sale of your book – you as an individual or as a company? Note that if the bank details you entered on the previous page are for a company bank account, then the answer is Business, even if you are the sole owner of that business.

Step 9:

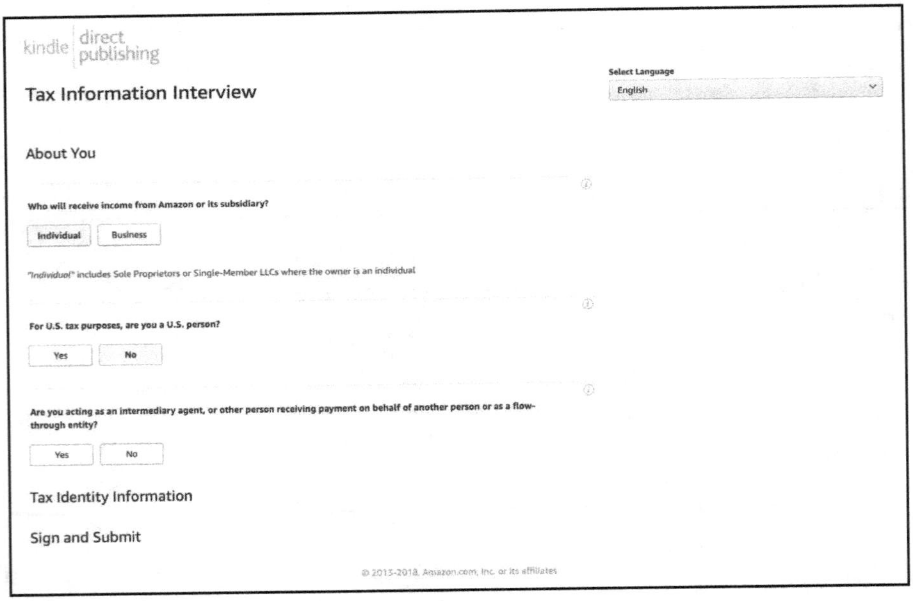

kindle direct publishing
Tax Information Interview
Select Language
English
About You
Who will receive income from Amazon or its subsidiary?
Individual
Business
"Individual" includes Sole Proprietors or Single-Member LLCs where the owner is an individual
For U.S. tax purposes, are you a U.S. person?
Yes
No
Are you acting as an intermediary agent, or other person receiving payment on behalf of another person or as a flow-through entity?
Yes
No
Tax Identity Information
Sign and Submit
© 2013-2018, Amazon.com, Inc. or its affiliates

Next, select whether for tax purposes you are a resident of the United States or not. You will then be asked if you are acting as an intermediary agent. If you will be passing on any royalty proceeds to another person, then the answer is Yes; if not it's No.

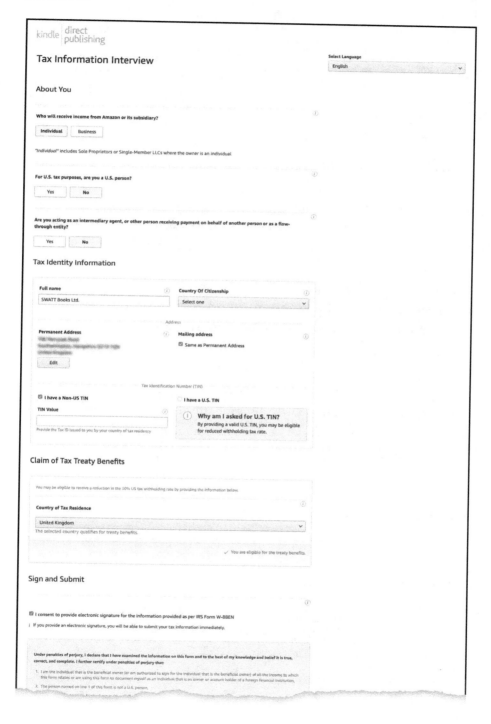

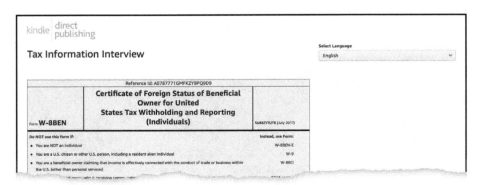

3. The income to which this form relates is: (a) not effectively connected... ...duct of a trade or business in the United States, (b) effectively connected but is not subject to tax under an applicable income tax treaty, or (c) the partner's share of a partnership's effectively connected income.

4. The person named on line 1 of this form is a resident of the treaty country listed on line 9 of the form (if any) within the meaning of the income tax treaty between the United States and that country.

5. For broker transactions or barter exchanges, the beneficial owner is an exempt foreign person as defined in the instructions, and

6. I agree that I will submit a new form within 30 days if any certification made on this form becomes incorrect.

Furthermore, I authorize this form to be provided to any withholding agent that has control, receipt, or custody of the income of which I am the beneficial owner or any withholding agent that can disburse or make payments of the income of which I am the beneficial owner.

The Internal Revenue Service does not require your consent to any provisions of this document other than the certifications required to establish your status as a non-U.S. individual and, if applicable, obtain a reduced rate of withholding.

Signature (Type your full name)

By typing my name on the given date, I acknowledge I am signing the tax documentation under penalties of perjury.

Date

05-20-2019

Save and Preview

© 2013-2018, Amazon.com, Inc. or its affiliates

You will then be asked to complete Tax Identity Information. Note that if you are a resident of the United Kingdom, select "I have a Non-US TIN" under Tax Identity Number and enter your National Insurance number.

Also be sure to check whether your country of residence appears in the dropdown list under Claim of Tax Treaty Benefits. If it does, it's important that you select this, as this ensures that you will not have to pay 30% US tax on any royalty earnings that your book makes.

Once you click Confirm, you will be asked to electronically sign a declaration that all of the information you have just submitted is accurate to the best of your knowledge. If so, type your name and the date at the bottom of the screen, then click **SAVE AND PREVIEW** .

Step 10:

kindle direct publishing

Tax Information Interview

Select Language

English

Reference Id: A0787771GMFKZY8PQ9D9

	Certificate of Foreign Status of Beneficial Owner for United States Tax Withholding and Reporting (Individuals)	
Form **W-8BEN**		SUBSTITUTE (July 2017)

Do NOT use this form if:	Instead, use Form:
• You are NOT an individual	W-8BEN-E
• You are a U.S. citizen or other U.S. person, including a resident alien individual	W-9
• You are a beneficial owner claiming that income is effectively connected with the conduct of trade or business within the U.S. (other than personal services)	W-8ECI

the U.S. (other than personal services)

- You are a beneficial owner who is receiving compensation for personal services performed in the United States .... 8233 or W-4
- A person acting as an intermediary W-8IMY

Part I Identification of Beneficial Owner

1 Name of individual who is the beneficial owner
SWATT Books Ltd.

2 Country of citizenship
United Kingdom

3 Permanent residence address (street, apt. or suite no., or rural route). Do not use a P.O. box or in-care-of address.
106 Merryoak Road

City or town, state or province. Include postal code where appropriate.
Southampton Hampshire SO19 7DN

Country
United Kingdom

4 Mailing address (if different from above)

City or town, state or province. Include postal code where appropriate.

Country

5 U.S. taxpayer identification number (SSN or ITIN), if required (see instructions)

6 Foreign tax identifying number (see instructions)

Part II Claim of Tax Treaty Benefits

9 I certify that the beneficial owner is a resident of United Kingdom within the meaning of the income tax treaty between the United States and that country.

10 Special rates and conditions (if applicable—see instructions): The beneficial owner is claiming the provisions of Article and paragraph 12(1) of the treaty identified on line 9 above to claim a 0.0% rate of withholding on (specify type of income): Royalty .

Explain the additional conditions in the Article and paragraph the beneficial owner meets to be eligible for the rate of withholding:

Part III Certification

Under penalties of perjury, I declare that I have examined the information on this form and to the best of my knowledge and belief it is true, correct, and complete. I further certify under penalties of perjury that:

1. I am the individual that is the beneficial owner (or am authorized to sign for the individual that is the beneficial owner) of all the income to which this form relates or am using this form to document myself for chapter 4 purposes,
2. The person named on line 1 of this form is not a U.S. person,
3. The income to which this form relates is (a) not effectively connected with the conduct of a trade or business in the United States, (b) effectively connected but is not subject to tax under an income tax treaty, or (c) the partner's share of a partnership's effectively connected income,
4. The person named on line 1 of this form is a resident of the treaty country listed on line 9 of the form (if any) within the meaning of the income tax treaty between the United States and that country, and
5. For broker transactions or barter exchanges, the beneficial owner is an exempt foreign person as defined in the instructions.

Furthermore, I authorize this form to be provided to any withholding agent that has control, receipt, or custody of the income of which I am the beneficial owner or any withholding agent that can disburse or make payments of the income of which I am the beneficial owner. I agree that I will submit a new form within 30 days if any certification made on this form becomes incorrect.

Sign Here   Samantha Pearce   03-29-2018

Signature of beneficial owner (or individual authorized to sign for beneficial owner)   Date (MM-DD-YYYY)   Capacity in which acting

Above is preview of your tax form based on the information you have provided. Please review and submit the form, or make changes if needed.

Make Changes   Submit Form

© 2015-2018, Amazon.com, Inc. or its affiliates

You will then be taken to a preview of the completed W-8BEN form that will be submitted to the IRS (the United States Internal Revenue Service). Review that all the information on it is correct and then sign and date the form at the bottom of the page before clicking **SUBMIT FORM** .

Step 11:

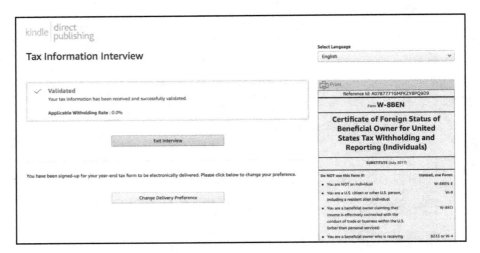

KDP will run an instant validation check on the tax information that you have supplied, after which you will see a screen confirming the amount of tax that you will be obliged to pay. You can then click **EXIT INTERVIEW** to be taken back to your account information page.

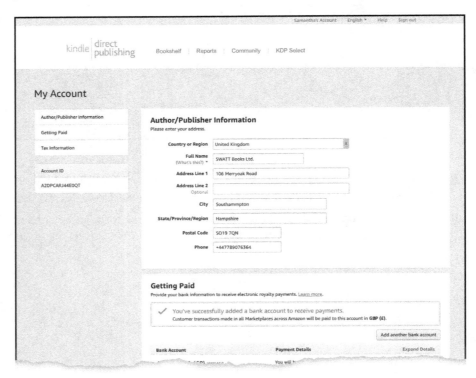

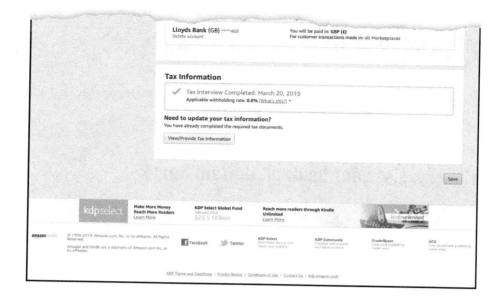

Click **SAVE** and you're done. You can then go to your Bookshelf to have a look around.

kindle | direct publishing   Bookshelf | Reports | Community | KDP Select

(i) CreateSpace is moving to Kindle Direct Publishing
If you have books on CreateSpace, move them to KDP in three steps. After you move your books, learn how to complete common tasks on KDP.

Create a New Title

+ Kindle eBook

- Book Content: You can upload a manuscript, or use our free creation tools to create children's books, educational content, comics, and manga. Get started with Kindle content creation tools.
- Book Cover: You can use our online Cover Creator, or upload a cover of your own. Creating a great cover.
- Description, Keywords and Categories: Tell readers about your book and help them find it on Amazon.
- ISBN: Get a free ISBN to publish your paperback. Kindle eBooks don't need one. More about ISBNs.

+ Paperback

See all Getting Started tips ›

Your Books

Sort by: Last Modified   Filter by: All   🔍 Title, status, etc.   Search

(i) Once you create a book it will show up here in your Bookshelf

10 Per Page ▾

PHASE 4: Listing your book

Once your accounts are set up, you are ready to create a new listing for your book.

How To: List your book on Ingram Spark

Start by clicking the **ADD A NEW TITLE** button at the top left of your Ingram Spark Dashboard.

Step 1:

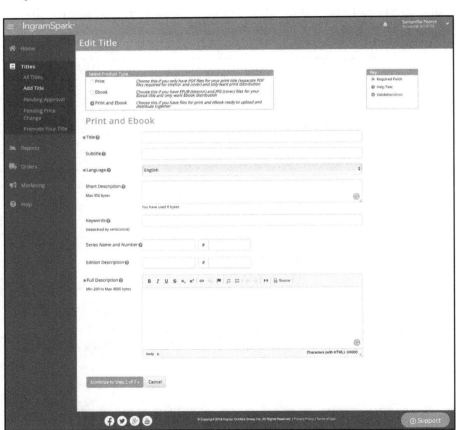

Begin by selecting the product type for your book – are you publishing a print book, an eBook, or both? The most common product type will be to select publishing both a print edition and an eBook so that is what we will base this tutorial on. Now proceed to fill in the relevant information. Only the information marked with a red * is required; however, I recommend that you complete as much of the additional information for the listing as possible, as it will make your book easier for readers to find, and appear more professional when presented on retail sites. Refer back to the Metadata section on page 68 for more guidance on making the most of your description and keywords.

1. **Title** – the main title of your book as you want it to appear.

2. **Subtitle** – this is any subtitle that you want to appear alongside your main title. This is particularly useful if you have opted for a short, catchy, more creative main title, as this acts as more of a descriptor of what the book is about i.e. Title: "The Intention Impact Conundrum" and subtitle: "Practical ways to achieve the impact you want".

3. **Language** – this gives you the option of localised English (such as British or American) but is also useful if you will be publishing translations of your book into other languages.

4. **Short Description** – even though this is not required I would strongly recommend completing this section. Think of it as a slightly longer Twitter synopsis of your book. Make it short, snappy and to the point, as you only have 350 characters including spaces and punctuation.

5. **Keywords** – again, although not a required field, this is vital information to ensure that your book can be found online. Approach these keywords in the same way that you select keywords for website SEO. Think about what terms your reader will use to search for your book and list them as individual words or short keyword phrases separated by a ";".

6. **Series Name & #** – this only applies if you are publishing a set of books in a series, such as a fictional trilogy or a how-to box set.

7. **Edition Description** – not required if this is the first time you have published this book, but if you are publishing a new edition to a previously published book then you would note that here.

8. **Full Description** – this is your complete book synopsis. Most authors will reproduce here the text from the back cover of the book jacket, along with a short testimonial or endorsement if available. You have a maximum of 4000 characters (including spaces and all punctuation), but you can also make use of formatting to make it easier to read and make it stand out.

Once all information has been submitted, click **CONTINUE TO STEP 2 OF 7** .

Step 2:

Next you will need to add information about the contributors to your book. As a minimum, you need to add your own details as the author, but you can also include details of anyone else who played a major role in the writing of the book, up to a maximum of three people. Be sure to click on the "About Contributor"

button next to each name you add so that you can supply additional information such as their biography and other published works.

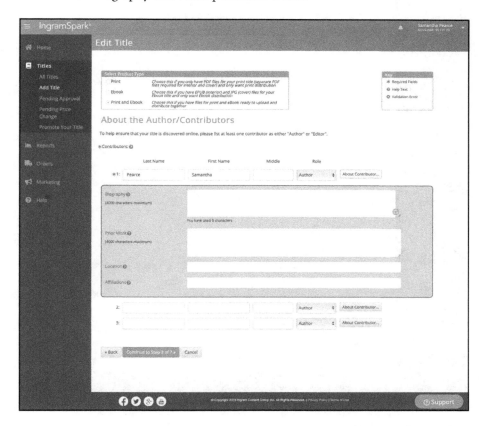

When all your contributors have been added, click on **CONTINUE TO STEP 3 OF 7** .

Step 3:

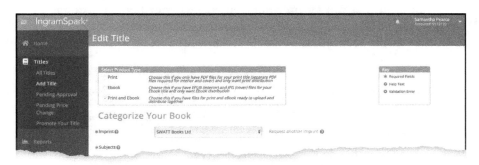

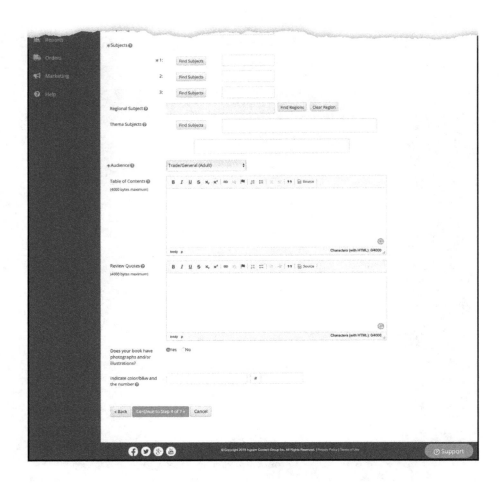

Now you are going to start to categorise your book. This informs retail channels what category(s) your book is to be listed under. Refer back to the Metadata section on page 68 for more guidance on selecting the best categories for your book.

1. **Imprint** – As a default, this will already be filled in with the name of the imprint that you set up when you opened your Ingram Spark account. However, you can request another one be linked to your account if you wish.

2. **Subjects** – Ingram Spark currently uses the BIC Subject Category system. You can find out more about this category system here: http://www.bic.org.uk/7/BIC-Standard-Subject-Categories, as well as using their handy Category Selection Tool. The easiest way to fill in this

section is to click the "Find Subject" button next to each subject field and search for one of the main keywords you entered into screen 1. Note that you can only select a maximum of three subjects, and I would order them from the most relevant first.

3. **Regional Subject** – If your book deals with a subject pertaining to a specific geographical region, then enter that information here. If not, leave it blank.

4. **Thema Subjects** – some online retailers are moving to the Thema subject classification system, a new global system which is beginning to gather wide international participation. You can find out more about the Thema classification system here: https://www.editeur.org/151/thema. Similar to section two above, click "Find Subject" and enter in one of your main keywords to find the relevant subject category.

5. **Audience** – select from the dropdown menu the audience that is most appropriate for your book. Unless you are publishing either a children's book or a book intended for academic use, the most common audience selection is General Adult Trade.

6. **Table of Contents** – when you pick up a book in a bookstore you generally flick through the book to browse the contents. However, when purchasing a book online, you are unable to do that, so supplying a copy of your table of contents is a great online selling tool. Simply copy and paste your table of contents here, deleting the page numbers to save on the number of characters you are using, as you are limited to 4000.

7. **Review Quotes** – reviews and endorsements are great selling tools for your book, as they provide social proof that your book is worth reading. If you have received any reviews or endorsements from advance readers or from reaction to editing copies, copy them here. Again, remember that you are limited to 4000 characters, so only submit the best ones.

8. If your book contains any photography or illustrations, select Yes and provide details as to roughly how many are included and whether they are black & white or full colour.

When ready, click **CONTINUE TO STEP 4 OF 7** .

Step 4:

This is where you will confirm the print specification of your hard copy book. Most of these details should have been thought about and discussed with your designer at the beginning of the book design process. Simply transfer that information here, including all these details:

> Trim size
> Interior pages printed in black & white or colour
> Paper stock you would like to use – white or cream
> Book to be bound as a paperback or hardback
> Print finish required for the cover
> Total page count, not including the cover

Then click **CONTINUE TO STEP 5 OF 7** .

Step 5:

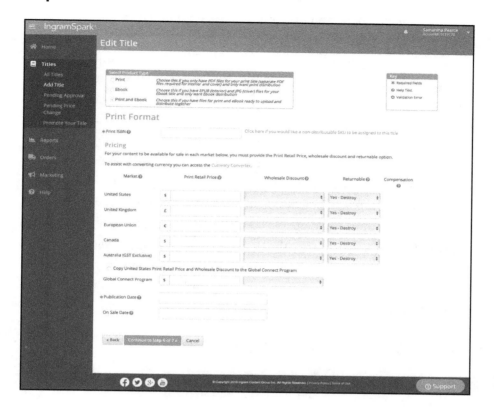

Now that you have supplied Ingram Spark with the print specification, we can now work out what the pricing should be for your print book.

Start off by entering the ISBN number that you are assigning to the print edition of your book. Then for each market where you want your book to be available, enter your recommended retail price. Note that retailers do not need to adhere to this cover price, but it will be used to calculate your royalty compensation. Next to each market cover price, select the wholesale discount that you are willing to offer to retailers who sell your book. The dropdown menu offers two options – 55% or Custom. I advise my authors to start with a wholesale discount of 45%; it gives the bulk of the profits to you as the author, but still provides enough margin for the retailer to make it worth their while listing your book. Once you have entered those two figures, Ingram Spark will calculate how much royalty you will earn in compensation for each book sold. You can adjust these figures to achieve the compensation amount that you require, but if you change the retail price, be sure to update it on the cover artwork if it is listed there.

You can also specify whether you will allow retailers to return your book if the reader, in turn, returns it to the retailer. If you are prepared to accept returns, you have the option of requesting the book be physically returned to you or destroyed.

Lastly, select your Publication Date. This is the official date that your book will be published, which is traditionally on a Thursday. You also have the option of setting a specific On Sale Date that is different from your publication date. This is useful if you want to build up to a book launch event, as this will allow readers to pre-order your book ahead of the launch. Any pre-orders will then be released on the On Sale Date. This can provide a very useful boost to your recorded book sales on your launch date, a great way to help you to achieve Amazon bestseller status.

Once complete, click **CONTINUE TO STEP 6 OF 7** .

Step 6:

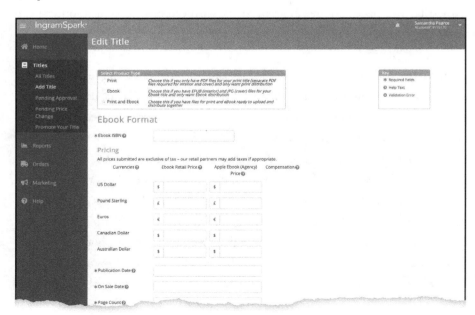

Step 6 replicates the process from Step 5 but with your eBook edition. Note that there are two separate retail price fields. This is because Apple iBooks insist on only accepting book prices ending in .99. Because of this, I would recommend that you set your eBook pricing to match the Apple iBooks pricing requirement so that you can list your eBook at the same price regardless of retailer.

It is worth noting that within the UK, eBooks are subject to VAT. This tax is added at the point of retail sale and NOT here, so bear in mind that once your book is listed, any cover price you enter here will have VAT added on top.

You will also notice that there is no option to set your preferred wholesale discount. This is because the wholesale discount for eBooks is a fixed amount set by Ingram Spark as a cost of distribution. At the time of publication of this book, the rate was 60%.

As a general rule, I would set your Publication Date and On Sale Date (if applicable) to be the same as your print edition; however, you can set them differently if you want to launch them separately.

Once ready to proceed, click **CONTINUE TO STEP 7 OF 7**.

Step 7:

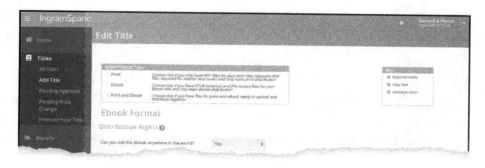

The last step in setting up your eBook is to confirm whether you have the rights to sell your eBook anywhere in the world. If you are the author and own the rights to the book in its entirety, then you have the right to distribute your book to any market where it is appropriate for your book to be sold. Yes is selected by default; if you change the dropdown menu to No, you will then be given the option to select which region(s) or territory(s) in which you wish to make your eBook available.

Once ready, click **CONTINUE** .

Step 8:

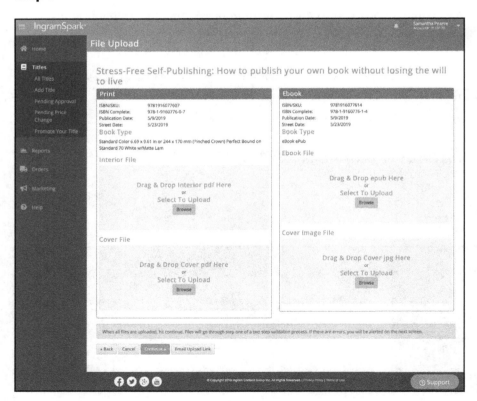

Now we get down to the business end of your book listing by uploading the artwork for your book.

Simply use the "Browse" button to select or 'drag and drop' each relevant file into the space reserved for the print interior and cover, as well as the eBook ePub file and cover image.

Once everything has uploaded successfully, click "Continue" and Ingram Spark will perform an automated validation check of your artwork to ensure that there are no immediately apparent issues with the files and that they comply with Ingram Spark specifications.

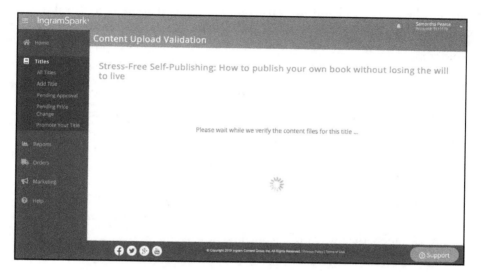

Step 9:

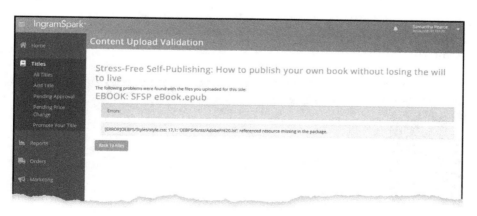

If any errors do get flagged up, you will be presented with a screen like the one above.

Ingram Spark will list any immediate errors that must be fixed before you are able to continue. These usually relate to coding errors in the eBook ePub file which are preventing the eBook from rendering properly. Or it may be that the system has detected that the trim size of the artwork does not match the specifications given. The system will also list separately any errors that are not critical to the production of the book but may affect quality, such as image resolution or the colour mode used in the artwork.

If there are any critical errors, you will only be given the option to return to the previous screen. You will then need to upload revised artwork that will fix the issues. Simply return to step 8, replace the affected files and then resubmit.

If however the only errors are non-critical, you will also be given the option to continue despite the issues raised. Note that if you opt to continue despite non-critical issues being flagged in the artwork, that you accept the risk that these issues may affect the quality of the final book.

Once your artwork has passed validation, you will be taken to the Setup Charges screen.

Step 10:

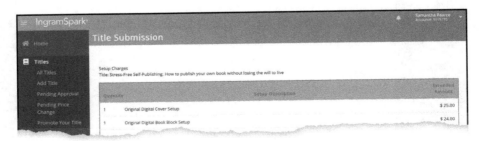

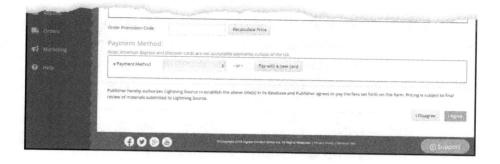

Here, Ingram Spark will list all of the setup charges pertaining to the listing of your book. If you have a promotional code, such as the one supplied to paid members of the Alliance of Independent Authors (ALLi), you can enter it here.

For the payment method, you have the option of paying using the debit or credit card that is saved to your Ingram Spark account, or you can opt to pay with a new card.

Once you have entered in either the security code for your saved card or provided the details for a new debit/credit card, click **I AGREE** to provide your authorisation for Lightning Source (who own Ingram Spark) to proceed with listing your book in its database.

Step 12:

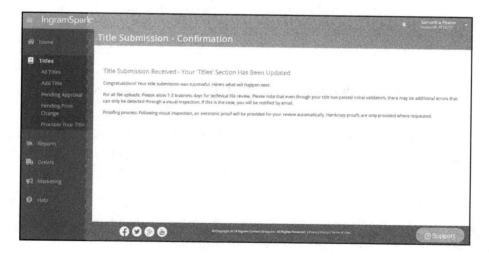

And that's it! Your book will now be sent for a final technical review by Ingram Spark's production team. This usually takes 1-2 business days, after which you will be notified by email either that there was a problem with your artwork or that your artwork is ready for final approval.

A note about eBook distribution

It is important to note that as soon as an eBook file passes the technical review stage with Ingram Spark's production team, it is automatically authorised for distribution to online retail channels such as the Apple iBooks, Kobo, and Nook stores.

This is why I recommend that you set your Publication Date and On Sale Date for eBooks and print editions to be the same date, as this avoids your book becoming public before your print edition is available to order.

How To: Approve your eProof on Ingram Spark

Once you have received the email indicating that your proof is ready to approve, log back into your Ingram Spark Dashboard. Click on the Titles Tab, and then on "Pending Approval" from the left-hand menu.

Step 1:

Select the title of your book from the list.

Step 2:

In the Title Approval screen, you have the option to download a PDF proof of your book artwork. I would recommend doing this, so that you have a record of the artwork file as Ingram Spark lists it, just in case you need it.

You then have four possible Proof Actions that you can take:

1. You approve the title and authorise Ingram Spark to release the book for distribution. This will trigger the print edition listing to be submitted to online retailers for inclusion in their catalogues immediately.

2. You approve the title, but DON'T authorise Ingram Spark to release the book for distribution. This is useful if you are planning on using your book as a client-only incentive and just want to take advantage of the print-on-demand model.

3. You reject the proof and request to provide new artwork.

4. You reject the proof and request Ingram Spark review the book further; for example, you suspect an export issue. In this instance, provide as much detail as possible in the text box provided, indicating the issue and where you want Ingram Spark to concentrate their review.

If you selected either of the two first options, I recommend checking the box at the bottom of the page and providing your email address. This will mean that a record of your approval of the book will be emailed to you for future reference.

For now, select option 2, then click **CONTINUE** and you will be taken back to the Ingram Spark Dashboard. This gives you the time to order and review a test copy of the book before it is released for distribution.

How To: List your book on KDP (Amazon)

Step 1:

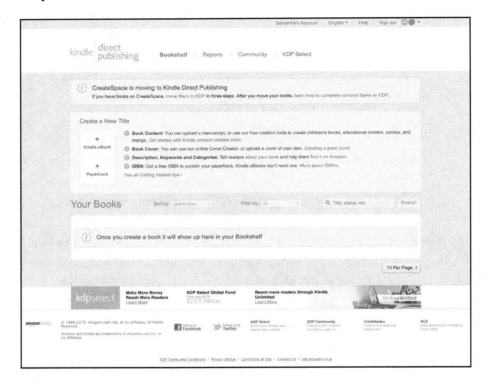

Log into your Amazon KDP account. Start by clicking the **+ KINDLE EBOOK** button in the "Create a New Title" section of your KDP Dashboard.

Step 2:

Language

Choose your ~~primary~~ language (the language in which the book was ~~written~~). Kindle. ▾

> English ⇕

Book Title

Enter your title as it will appear on the book cover.

Book Title

> _____

Subtitle (Optional)

> _____

Series

The series name and volume number will help customers find other books in your series on Amazon.

Series Information (Optional)

> Series name   Series number

Edition Number

You can provide an edition number if this title is a new edition of an existing book. What counts as a new edition? ▾

Edition Number (Optional)

> _____

Author

Primary Author or Contributor

> First name   Last name

Contributors

Contributors (Optional)

> Author ⇕   First name   Last name   Remove

> Add Another

Description

This will appear on your book's Amazon detail page. Why do book descriptions matter? ▾

>
>
>

4000
characters left

Publishing Rights

○ I own the copyright and I hold the necessary publishing rights. What are publishing rights? ▾

○ This is a public domain work. What is a public domain work? ▾

Keywords

Enter up to 7 search keywords that describe your book. How do I choose keywords? ▾

Your Keywords (Optional)

> _____   _____

> _____   _____

> _____   _____

> _____

Categories

Choose up to two browse categories. Why are categories important? ▾

> Set Categories

Age and Grade Range

Children's book age range (Optional)

Age Range

Minimum   Maximum

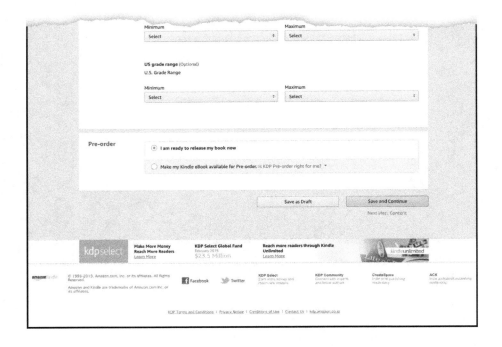

You will then be taken to the Kindle eBook Details screen where you will enter all the details about your eBook. You should use all of the same information that you included in your Ingram Spark book listing.

1. Language

2. Book Title, and any applicable subtitle

3. Whether the book is part of a series (leave blank if it is not).

4. Edition number

5. First and last name of the primary author

6. Any additional authors or contributors that require mentioning in the book listing

7. Description. This is the main synopsis of your book that will appear on its Amazon detail page. Note that you have a 4,000-character limit.

8. Declaration of whether you own the publishing rights to the book or if it is a public domain work.

9. Keywords. You can enter up to 7 separate keywords or keyword phrases to describe your book. It helps to think about what your readers would search for to find your book.

10. Categories that you want your book to appear under. You can choose two.

11. Age and Grade Range. Note that this is only applicable if you are publishing a children's book.

12. Whether you want to have your Kindle eBook available for pre-order or have it published straightaway.

Once completed, click **SAVE AND CONTINUE** .

Step 3:

Next you will be taken to the Kindle eBook Content page where you can upload the files associated with your eBook.

1. **Manuscript:** Select Upload eBook manuscript and select the ePub file supplied by your designer.

   > **DRM:** You will also need to decide whether you want Amazon's Digital Rights Management (DRM) feature enabled for your book. This is basically an extra layer of security to prohibit unauthorised access to or copying of digital content. It is worth noting that DRM will not prevent all piracy and does make it difficult for paying readers to access your book on multiple devices such as their Kindle and a Kindle reading app on their smartphone. Therefore, I suggest not enabling this feature, as many readers will not buy DRM-enabled

books, but it is up to you. Note that once selected, this option cannot be changed later.

2. **Cover:** You have the option to use the Kindle Cover Creator to make a cover for your book, but I would recommend uploading the JPEG of your print book cover using the "Upload your cover file" button.

3. **Online Preview:** Once you have uploaded all the content files for your eBook, I recommend launching the Online Previewer to review how your eBook will look once readers download it. Note that the process of converting your files can take several minutes, so be patient.

4. **ISBN:** Enter in the ISBN number associated with your eBook.

Once all information has been filled in and you are happy with the results of the online preview, click "Save and Continue".

Step 4:

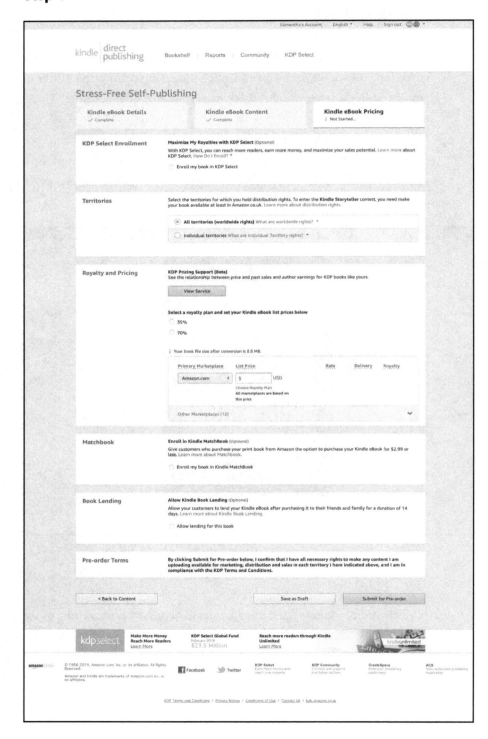

The final step of setting up your eBook is to enter your pricing.

1. **KDP Select:** Firstly, you have the option of enrolling your eBook in KDP Select. This option earns you a higher rate of royalty, but it does then tie your eBook into being exclusively available on the Kindle Store, meaning it cannot be listed anywhere else. As this book is based on a dual publishing model, I would suggest that you do not enrol in this feature.

2. **Territories:** You can select whether you want your eBook to be available worldwide or only in particular territories.

3. **Royalty & Pricing:** Here you can choose which royalty plan you wish to opt into – either 35% or 70%. You may be thinking "that's a no-brainer... why would anyone opt to take a lower royalty rate?", but there are pros and cons to each option that actually makes this decision a little bit more complicated. For example with the 70% royalty rate a delivery cost that is based on the file size of your eBook is deducted from your royalties before being paid, whereas that cost does not apply to the 35% rate. So give some thought to this before automatically selecting the 70% option. For a detailed breakdown of the pros and cons of each plan, please refer to the KDP Digital Pricing Page: https://kdp.amazon.com/en_US/help/ topic/G200634500. Once you have selected your royalty level, you can begin entering in the cover price of your book for each market. As you do so, KDP will automatically calculate the amount of royalty you will earn from sales in each territory.

4. **Matchbook:** This gives customers who purchase the print edition of your book the option to buy the Kindle edition at a reduced cost, usually $2.99 or less. I've not had any experience with this service; however research that I've done indicates that it's a service that has not been very well supported by Amazon.

5. **Book Lending:** This option allows you to submit your book to the Kindle Book Lending Programme. This means that readers who purchase your eBook are able to lend it to friends and family without them having to purchase it for a period of 14 days. Not every eBook qualifies for the

Kindle Book Lending Programme; however, if it does, this option will be available to select. Amazon have put safeguards in place to prevent abuse of this system, but it does potentially mean fewer paying sales for you if you opt in.

6. **Terms & Conditions:** Read through the KDP Terms and Conditions before proceeding. By clicking "Publish Your Kindle eBook" at the bottom of the page, you are confirming that you have all the necessary rights to the book and will comply with KDP Ts & Cs.

Step 4:

Once you have completed all sections, you have the option of either saving your eBook as a draft to be published later (recommended) or publishing it straightaway. By clicking **PUBLISH YOUR KINDLE EBOOK** , your book will be listed within 72 hours and available to purchase immediately. This is unless you opted for Kindle Pre-Order in Step 1.

I would recommend that you save your book as a draft until you have submitted all the details for your print edition and have received and approved a test copy. Then you can release both editions at the same time to coordinate with the on-sale date you have set on Ingram Spark.

Step 5:

Click **DONE** and you will be taken back to your KDP Dashboard where you can see your eBook saved as a Draft in the Your Books list.

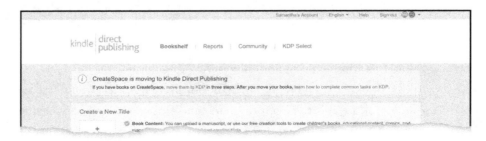

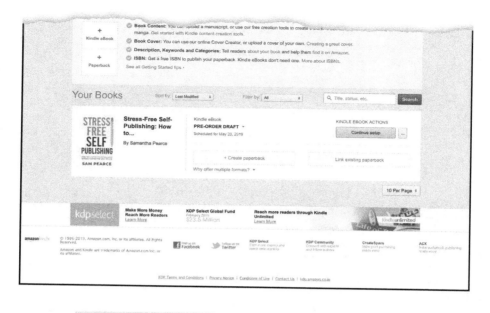

Click the **+ CREATE PAPERBACK** next to your eBook cover thumbnail to add the details for the paperback edition.

Step 6:

Edition Number   You can provide an edition number if this title is a new edition of an existing book. What counts as a new edition? *

Edition number (Optional)

[   ]

Author   Your paperback should have at least one author or primary contributor.

Primary Author or Contributor

| Prefix | Samantha | Middle name | Pearce | Suffix |

Contributors   You can add additional contributors including more authors, illustrators, editors, and translators, among others.

Contributors (Optional)

| Author ⋄ | Prefix | First name | Middle name | Last name | Suffix | Remove |

[Add Another]

Description   This will appear on your book's Amazon detail page. Why do book descriptions matter? *

Stress-Free Self-Publishing

Have you ever thought about self-publishing a book, but are unsure where to start or feel overwhelmed by conflicting

2982
characters left

Publishing Rights
- ● I own the copyright and I hold necessary publishing rights. What are publishing rights? *
- ○ This is a public domain work What is a public domain work? *

Keywords   Choose up to 7 keywords that describe your book. How do I choose keywords? *

Your Keywords (Optional)

Self publishing	Publish a book
KDP publishing	Independent publishing
Ingram Spark	How to self-publish
Amazon self publishing	

Categories   Choose up to two browse categories. Why are categories important? *

Nonfiction > Language Arts & Disciplines > Publishing
Nonfiction > Language Arts & Disciplines > Authorship

[Choose categories]

☐ Large print. What is large print? *

Adult Content   Does this book contain language, situations, or images inappropriate for children under 18 years of age?

- ● No
- ○ Yes

[Save as Draft]   [Save and Continue]

Next step: Content

Most of the title details will already be populated from the eBook edition. Check through them to make sure that they are all correct. The main section that will NOT be pre-populated will be the Categories section. This is because Kindle and print book categories differ on Amazon. Choose up to two categories that you want your print edition book to be listed under. You also need to declare whether your book contains any adult content. Once completed, click **SAVE AND CONTINUE** .

Step 7:

Next will be to supply all of the print specifications and upload the artwork files for the content of your paperback edition.

1. **ISBN:** Enter in the ISBN number for the print edition of your book. Do not opt to have Amazon assign a free KDP ISBN to your book, as this will result in Amazon being listed as the publisher for your book and not you.

2. **Publication Date:** This is only applicable for second editions or for books that have been previously published elsewhere. If your book falls into this category, enter in the date that your book was FIRST published.

3. **Print Options:** From the options, select the print specification for your book, including paper type, trim size, whether your book contains bleeds and what finish you would like on your cover.

4. **Manuscript:** Upload the print-ready PDF of your book interior artwork.

5. **Cover:** Upload the print-ready PDF of your cover jacket.

6. **Preview:** Once all your artwork has been uploaded, launch the Previewer to ensure that your artwork has uploaded correctly and complies with the print specification set. Note that the Amazon artwork requirement for front cover artwork differs slightly from Ingram Spark, so you may need to alter the artwork export settings slightly. Your cover designer will be able to help you with this if necessary.

Once you are happy with the Preview, click **APPROVE**. You will be taken back to the Paperback Pricing Screen; scroll to the bottom and click **SAVE AND CONTINUE**.

Step 8:

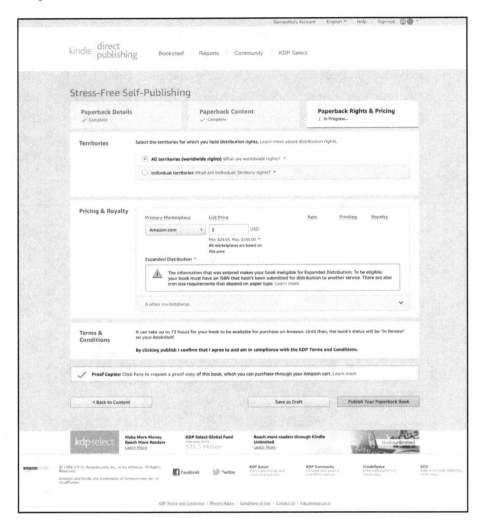

The last step in setting up your paperback edition is to set up your cover pricing.

1. **Territories:** First select whether you want your book available worldwide or just in selected territories.

2. **Pricing & Royalty:** Then enter in the list price for each major Amazon territory. KDP will automatically calculate the royalty you will earn from each copy sold in each territory. KDP will also check whether your book is eligible for Expanded Distribution. If the option is available, do NOT

select it, as Expanded Distribution is Amazon's version of distributing your book outside of Amazon, which will already be taken care of by Ingram Spark.

3. **Terms & Conditions:** Again, read through the KDP Terms & Conditions as these will differ from the eBook Ts & Cs you agreed to in the previous section.

Once you have completed all sections, click **CLICK HERE TO REQUEST A PROOF COPY**.

Step 9:

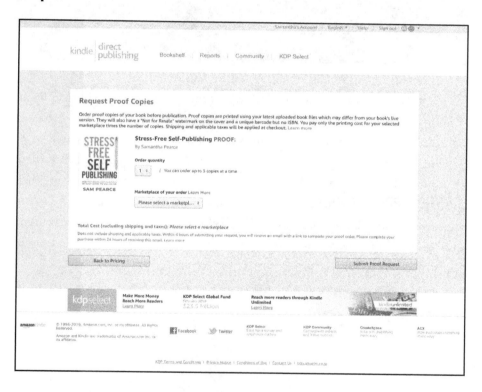

You now have the option of ordering up to five proof copies of your book to be printed and delivered to you for review before publishing. Select which marketplace that you want your books to be printed – for this choose the Amazon site you use regularly for purchases. Then click **SUBMIT PROOF REQUEST**.

Step 10:

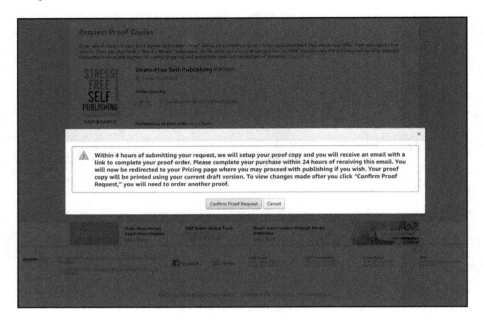

You will then see a notification window informing you that it will take up to 4 hours for your proof to be set up on the system. Once this process has been completed, you will receive an email with a link to complete the purchase of your test copies, which you can then do from your Amazon shopping cart. Note that you will only have 24 hours to complete your purchase. Once you click **CONFIRM PROOF REQUEST** you will be taken back to the Paperback Pricing page where you will then click **SAVE AS DRAFT** to save your book in draft mode until you have received your test copies to allow you to approve that you are happy with the results.

PHASE 5: Test print

It is advisable to also order a single test copy of your print book from Ingram Spark so that you can be 100% certain you are happy with what your reader will receive before you release your book for distribution.

How To: Order a test print from Ingram Spark

Step 1:

Log into your Ingram Spark account and click the **ACTION** drop down menu to the right of your title and select **ORDER** button for the print edition of your book. This is on the far right of your Dashboard.

You will then be taken to a pre-populated order screen.

Step 2:

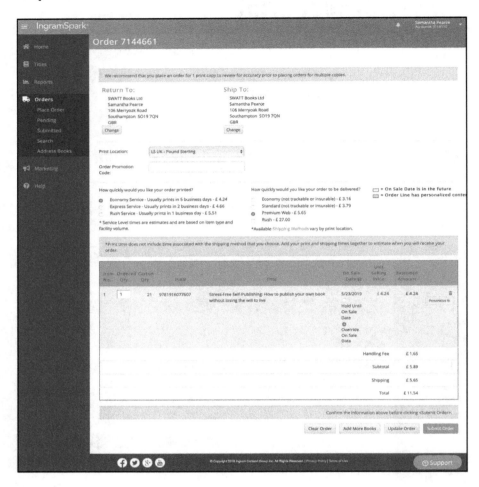

Once here, confirm your shipping address, how quickly you would like the order printed, and how quickly you would like the order shipped to you. I always recommend opting for the "Premium Web" delivery service, as this option is tracked and signed for via UPS, so you have a level of protection against your book getting lost in the post, which I have had happen before.

If you make any changes to the print or delivery service, make sure to click the **UPDATE ORDER** button at the bottom of the screen so that you are viewing the most up-to-date pricing.

Before proceeding, make sure you select the **OVERRIDE ON SALE DATE** radio button next to your book title.

Once you've confirmed that all the details are correct, click **SUBMIT ORDER** .

Step 3:

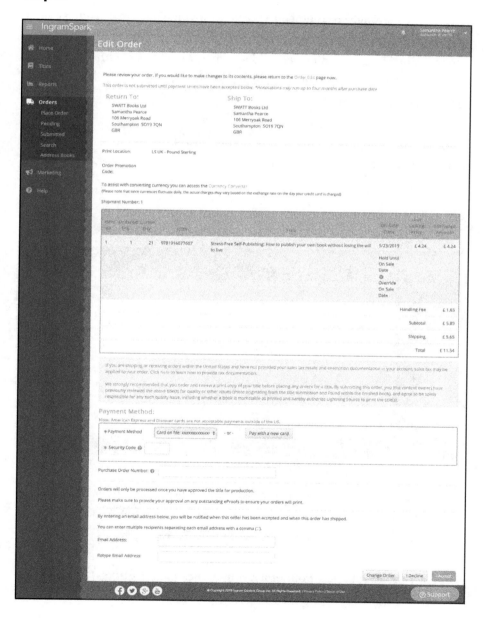

As with previous order screens, simply select whether you want to pay using the debit/credit card you have saved on your profile or enter in details of a new card.

I would recommend entering some kind of reference in the Purchase Order Number field so that you can easily find the order again should you need to search for it in future.

I would also strongly recommend that you provide your email address at the bottom of the screen before proceeding. By doing this, Ingram Spark will send you regular updates regarding your order such as when they confirm receipt, and when the order ships. This will also allow UPS to send you the tracking numbers for the delivery.

Once you are happy with everything, click **I ACCEPT** to place the order and allow Ingram Spark to take payment.

Step 4:

Once your payment has gone through, you will see an order confirmation screen listing your order number. Please do not click the **BACK** button on your browser, as this can sometimes trigger a duplicate card charge.

If you wish to refer back to your order, simply click on the **SUBMITTED ORDERS** tab in the left-hand side menu.

PHASE 6: Test copy review

When you receive your test copies, check them for print quality and that you are happy with the overall look and feel of the book. I would also recommend that you read through your book one last time. It is not uncommon for the odd mistake that has been missed to suddenly jump out at you now that your book is in a physical format. This is the last opportunity you will get to make changes to your book without incurring any amendment fees from the publishing platforms.

If you do need/want to make changes to the artwork before proceeding, simply log into your Ingram Spark account, click on the Title name of your book from the Dashboard, and click the **UPLOAD NEW ARTWORK** button at the top right of the book listing screen. Then repeat steps 8 through to 12 from the book listing tutorial. Don't forget, if you do make any amendments to content, to update your eBook files as well, and to update any revised artwork on KDP.

PHASE 7: Title release & PoD order

Once you are happy with your test prints, it is time to release your book for distribution.

How To: Release your book for distribution on Ingram Spark

Step 1:

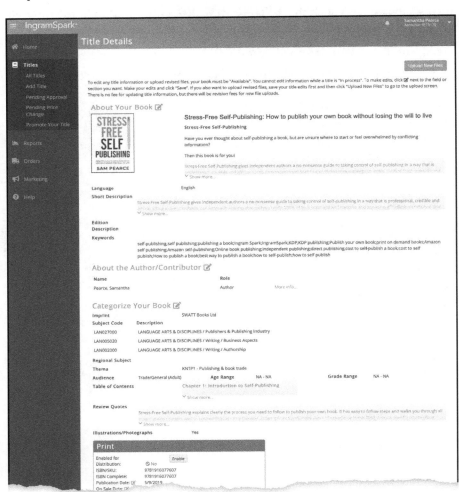

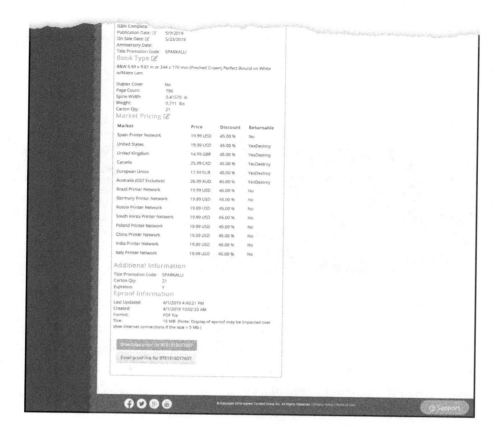

Sign into your Ingram Spark account, and once in your Dashboard click the print edition title of your book. You will be taken to the title information page.

Towards the bottom of the screen in the Print edition column, the first line reads "Enabled for Distribution" with a do not enter symbol next to it. Click where it says **ENABLE** .

Step 2:

You will be asked to confirm whether you are sure you want to enable distribution for this title. Click **YES** .

Step 3:

You will be given the option to "Promote" your title. Ingram Spark produces a quarterly magazine which they send out to their distribution network informing them of new books that have been published in the previous quarter. A listing in this magazine costs $85 USD. It is not mandatory but can be good for creating retail interest in your book ahead of launch.

Step 4:

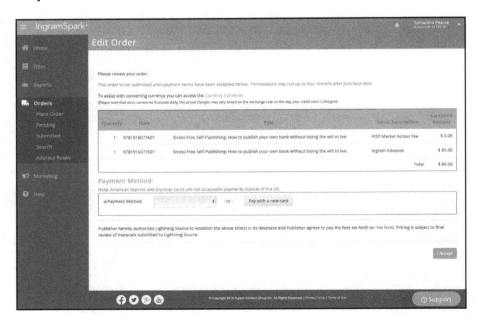

Releasing your book for distribution does trigger an order to be generated; however, rest assured that the process of releasing your book for distribution is free of charge. The main purpose of raising an order that you must approve is to ensure that you are giving full consent for Lightning Source to release your print edition book for distribution. Simply click **I ACCEPT** .

Step 5:

Once you click Accept, then you will be taken to a final order confirmation page and you are done – your book is now winging its way to online retailers ready to start selling!

How To: Release your book for distribution on KDP (Amazon)

You will want to do this step immediately after you release your book for distribution on Ingram Spark. If you wait too long, Ingram will have already submitted metadata for your book to Amazon and you could end up with duplicate listings.

Step 1:

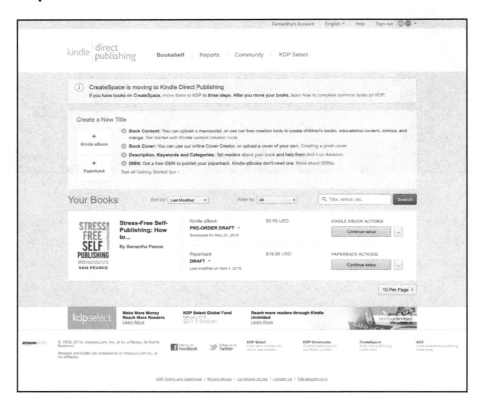

Log back into your KDP account and click on **BOOKSHELF** at the top of the screen to view your KDP Dashboard. Click on **CONTINUE SETUP** button under KINDLE EBOOK ACTIONS.

Step 2:

Skip to the last section by clicking the **KINDLE EBOOK PRICING** tab at the top of the page.

Step 3:

Scroll to the bottom of the page and click **PUBLISH YOUR KINDLE EBOOK** .

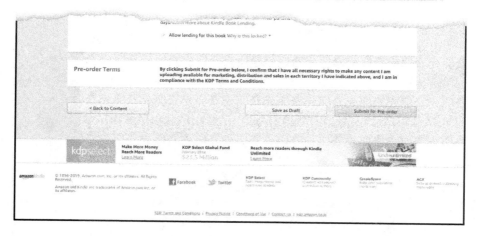

Step 4:

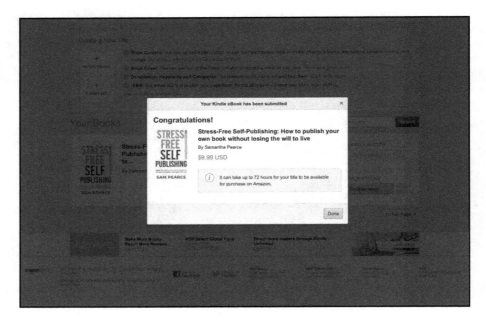

A congratulations window will pop up informing you that it will take up to 72 hours for your eBook listing to go live and be available for purchase on Amazon. Click "Done", and you'll be taken back to your KDP Dashboard, where you will repeat the same steps for your Paperback edition.

***

Now is also the time to order a batch of print books for your own sales and marketing purposes. These can be set up for sale through your own website or to clients, to give as gifts to friends and family, or to send out for review to journalists, review critics and book blogs. I recommend ordering your PoD copies from Ingram Spark, as their production fees tend to be a bit cheaper than Amazon, but it is always worth comparing to be certain.

How To: Place a PoD order on Ingram Spark

Step 1:

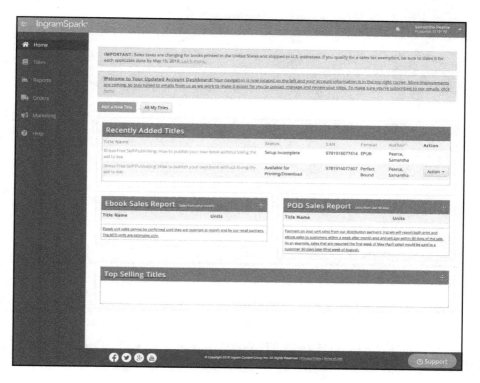

Log into your Ingram Spark account, and from your Dashboard click on the **ORDER** button next to your print book.

Step 2:

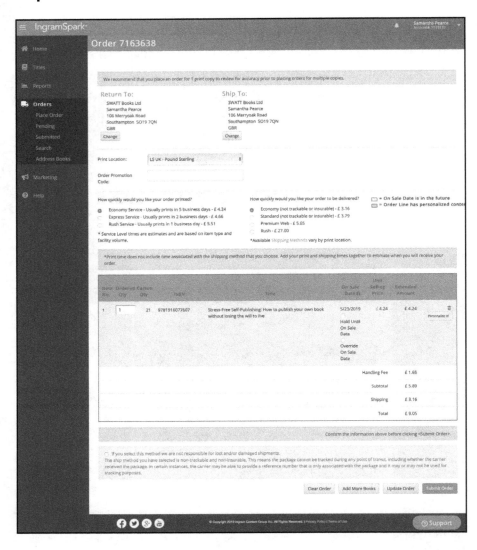

Once here, confirm your shipping address, how quickly you would like the order printed, and how quickly you would like the order shipped to you. Generally, if you are ordering more than five copies of your book, the two non-tracked delivery options will be removed, and the "Premium Web" option will be selected by default.

Step 3:

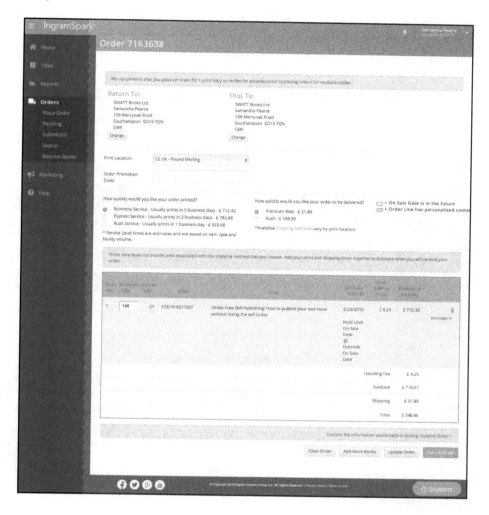

You also need to confirm the number of copies that you would like to order. It is more efficient to order full boxes of books, as this will ensure that you are not paying to ship empty air. Column 3 of the order sheet shows how many of your books fit into a single box (labelled 'Carton Qty'); ideally you want to order in multiples of this number, but of course, with print-on-demand, you can order any quantity you wish.

Once you have confirmed your order quantity, make sure you click the "Update Order" button at the bottom of the screen so that you are viewing the most up-to-date pricing.

Before proceeding, make sure you select the "Override On Sale Date" radio button (if applicable) next to your book title. If your official On Sale date has passed, then this option will not appear and the line listing for your book will not be highlighted in yellow.

Once you have confirmed that all the details are correct, click **SUBMIT ORDER**.

Step 4:

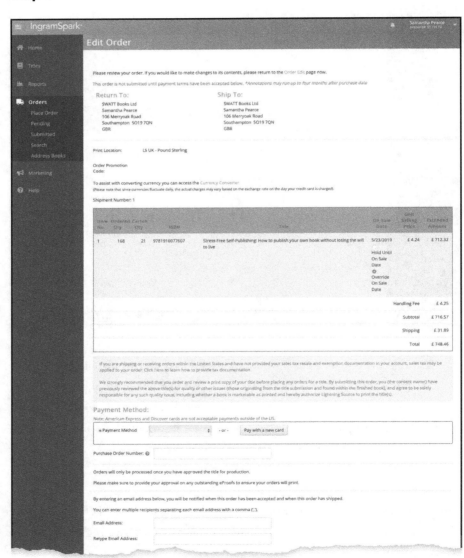

As with previous order screens, simply select whether you want to pay using the debit/credit card you have saved on your profile or enter in details of a new card.

I would recommend entering some kind of reference in the Purchase Order Number field so that you can easily find the order again should you need to search for it in future.

I would also highly recommend that you provide your email address at the bottom of the screen before proceeding. By doing this, Ingram Spark will send you regular updates regarding your order such as when they confirm receipt and when the order ships. This will also allow UPS to send you the tracking numbers for the delivery.

Once you are happy with everything, click **I ACCEPT** to place the order and allow Ingram Spark to take payment.

Step 5:

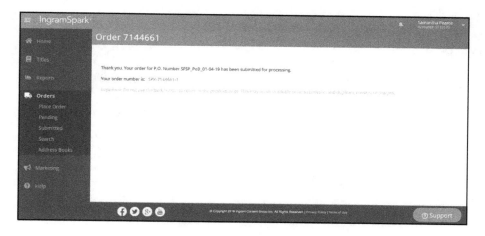

Once your payment has gone through, you'll see an order confirmation screen listing your order number. Make sure that you do not click the **BACK** button on your browser as this can sometimes trigger a duplicate card charge.

If you wish to refer back to your order, simply click on the **SUBMITTED ORDERS** tab in the left-hand side menu.

PHASE 8: Legal deposits & database listing

The last step in the process is to fulfil your legal deposit obligations. Most countries with a governing ISBN agency will require you to submit a printed copy of your book for public record as part of your ISBN agreement. In the UK, the British Library is the holder of all legal deposits and you are required by UK law to submit a printed copy of your book to them within six months of publication. See the British Library website for more details: https://www.bl.uk/legal-deposit

There are five other legal deposit libraries across the UK that are entitled to request a free copy of your book within one year of publication. These include the Bodleian Library at the University of Oxford, Cambridge University Library, the National Library of Scotland, the library of Trinity College, Dublin and the National Library of Wales. This process is usually coordinated jointly through the Agency for the Legal Deposit Libraries. Note that it is not a legal requirement for you to submit your book to these additional libraries straightaway. If they require a copy of your book, they will send you a request to submit your book, at which point you are then legally obliged to send them the required copies of your book within six weeks of receiving the request.

In the US, the National Library of Congress holds legal deposits (referred to as Mandatory Deposits in the US). As with the UK, legal deposit requirements are written into US law, and state that you must submit two copies of your book to the Copyright Office within three months of publication. See the US Copyright Office website for more details: https://www.copyright.gov/mandatory/

**

Congratulations! You are now technically a published author. Now you need to make sure that bricks & mortar bookstores can find your book should they wish to stock it. To do this, you need to complete a book database listing with your ISBN agency. This adds a record of your book to an international database of all allocated ISBN numbers and is used as a data feed into the majority of bookstore and book distributor ordering systems.

How To: Submit a listing to the Nielsen book database

First of all, you will need to sign up for a Nielsen Title Editor account. Note that this is different from the account that you set up to purchase your ISBN numbers.

Step 1:

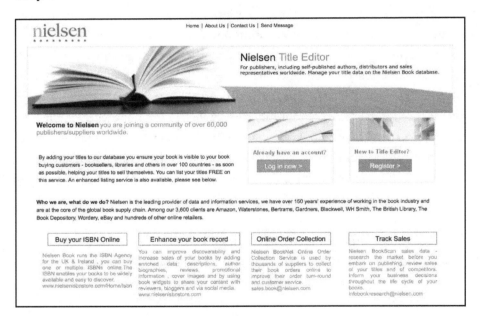

Go to https://www.nielsentitleeditor.com/titleeditor/ and click the grey **REGISTER** button in the top right corner of the page.

Step 2:

Nielsen Title Editor

For publishers, including self-published authors, distributors and sales
representatives worldwide. Manage your title data on the Nielsen Book database.

Nielsen BookData Title Editor Terms & Conditions

Title Editor is an online electronic title record editing service for Publishers, or data suppliers authorised to provide data on their behalf only. It is a free service offered to approved users.

Please note that access to the Title Editor service is at the discretion of Nielsen Book Services Ltd and that the company reserves the right to withdraw this service generally or to specific users if it is deemed necessary.

If you would like to find out more about our Nielsen BookData Enhanced Service for Publishers please
email: publisher.services.book@nielsen.com

DEFINITION: Nielsen BookData is a trading name of Nielsen Book Services Ltd ("NBSL")

INTERNET CHARGES: The additional costs of Internet use (Internet service provider subscription, call charges, etc) are the responsibility of the user.

"Title Editor user" or "user" means the business, or business unit to which a username is allocated. This term is also used to define any Sales Agent, or Publisher acting as a sales agent on behalf of another publisher, or Distributor authorised to provide local Price and Availability information on behalf of publishers, who is also authorised to use Title Editor.

"We", "us", or "our" means Nielsen Book Services Limited, trading as Nielsen BookData, 3rd Floor, Midas House, 62 Goldsworth Road, Woking, Surrey GU21 6LQ, UK.

If you have any queries about these terms and conditions, please contact one of our Sales and Customer Service teams:

UK +44 (0)1483 712 200 or email: sales.bookdata@nielsen.com
Australia 1800 683 522 or email: sales@nielsenbookdata.com.au
New Zealand +64 9 360 3294 or email: sales@nielsenbookdata.co.nz
Asia Pacific +64 9 360 3294 or email: info@nielsenbookdata.biz

By becoming a user of Title Editor, you accept the following terms and conditions.

Access to the Title Editor site is controlled by username and password. All Usernames and Passwords are issued to a designated, named contact as a representative of a distinct business unit, usually a company, but may, by arrangement, be a discrete trading division within a company, where appropriate. Usernames may be used by multiple individuals, authorised to provide data on behalf of the business unit, but not concurrently.

Confidentiality: Title Editor Users shall keep all log-on details (Username, Password) secure and confidential, and undertake that such log-on details will only be used by the Publisher and its employees and that they will not be passed to any third parties.

In addition, the Title Editor service is provided as a means to supply product information for inclusion in NBSL data products and services. Copyright in the complete product database used in the Title Editor web site and its design is held by NBSL. You must not copy the web site, or any of its pages, for any purpose whatsoever unless we have given you permission in writing to do so.

Provision of product information to NBSL through Title Editor is covered by Nielsen BookData's Standard Terms and Conditions for Publishers or, in the case of organisations subscribing to Nielsen BookData's Enhanced Service, our Standard Terms and Conditions for Subscribing Publishers .

Data changes you submit via Title Editor are applied to the central Nielsen Bibliographic database **by our editorial staff** and these changes will then be reflected in the next available data products we supply to external website customers, our range of products and services, and Nielsen Title Editor itself. Changes made by Publishers subscribing to our Nielsen BookData Enhanced Service will **normally** be applied to the Bibliographic database within 24 hours and available to view on Title Editor again within 3 working days. Changes made by non-subscribing publishers on the Free Listing service may take up to 2 weeks to be visible within Title Editor. Wilful provision of inappropriate product information (where we consider that it may be unlawful, fraudulent, libellous, defamatory or obscene) may lead to termination of user access to Title Editor.

Accuracy and limitation of liability: We use all reasonable efforts to ensure the accuracy and proper operation of Title Editor, but we cannot guarantee that errors will not occur, or accept responsibility for the consequences of such errors. Our total liability will be limited to a refund of the whole or part of a current Enhanced Service data subscription (see above) or an extension of the subscription term. We welcome feedback if you have found any error and we will try to correct such errors, where we are able to verify, which you notify to us within a reasonable time.

We use all reasonable efforts to ensure that Title Editor is kept free from computer viruses or other potentially harmful content, but we cannot guarantee that the service will always be clear of contamination. It is your responsibility to take appropriate measures to protect your own systems.

Force majeure: We are not responsible to you for any interruption to or delay in access to the Title Editor web site which is caused by reasons outside our control.

Non-transferability: You must not transfer your user access to Title Editor to any third party unless we have given you permission in writing to do so.

Data Protection: All contact and address information relating to publisher, agent or distribution details are deemed as company rather than personal information. Users are advised that personal details (such as personal email addresses) are better avoided: generic/proxy, more persistent addresses (such as sales@publisher etc) are better.

Changes to these terms and conditions: We reserve the right to make changes to these terms and conditions at any time, and will notify users with advance notice of such changes.

Termination: We may terminate your access to Title Editor without notice if you have not complied with any of these terms and conditions. We will write to you setting out our reasons for doing so. We will be under no obligation to refund any unused portion of your publisher subscription in ···ircumstances.

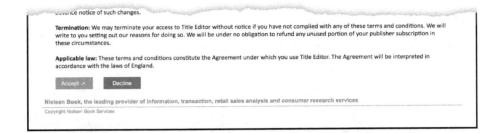

notice of such changes.

Termination: We may terminate your access to Title Editor without notice if you have not complied with any of these terms and conditions. We will write to you setting out our reasons for doing so. We will be under no obligation to refund any unused portion of your publisher subscription in these circumstances.

Applicable law: These terms and conditions constitute the Agreement under which you use Title Editor. The Agreement will be interpreted in accordance with the laws of England.

Accept >   Decline

Nielsen Book, the leading provider of information, transaction, retail sales analysis and consumer research services

Read through to the Nielsen Book Data Title Editor Terms & Conditions, then click **ACCEPT** to continue.

Step 3:

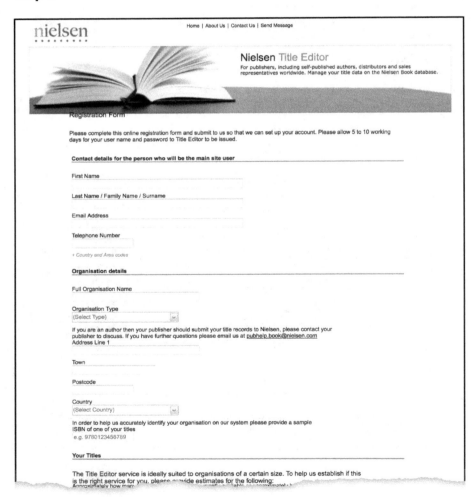

nielsen

Home | About Us | Contact Us | Send Message

Nielsen Title Editor

For publishers, including self-published authors, distributors and sales representatives worldwide. Manage your title data on the Nielsen Book database.

Registration Form

Please complete this online registration form and submit to us so that we can set up your account. Please allow 5 to 10 working days for your user name and password to Title Editor to be issued.

Contact details for the person who will be the main site user

First Name

Last Name / Family Name / Surname

Email Address

Telephone Number

+ Country and Area codes

Organisation details

Full Organisation Name

Organisation Type
(Select Type)

If you are an author then your publisher should submit your title records to Nielsen, please contact your publisher to discuss. If you have further questions please email us at pubhelp.book@nielsen.com
Address Line 1

Town

Postcode

Country
(Select Country)

In order to help us accurately identify your organisation on our system please provide a sample ISBN of one of your titles
e.g. 9780123456789

Your Titles

The Title Editor service is ideally suited to organisations of a certain size. To help us establish if this is the right service for you, please provide estimates for the following:
Approximately how man

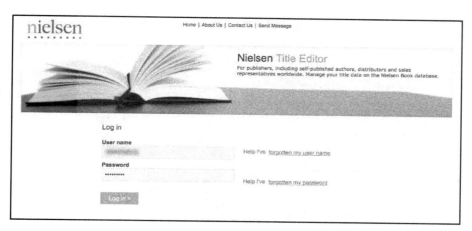

Your Titles

The Title Editor service is ideally suited to organisations of a certain size. To help us establish if this is the right service for you, please provide estimates for the following:
Approximately how many of your publications are currently available or approximately how many unique ISBNs is your organisation responsible for that are currently on sale?

In the coming year, approximately how many unique ISBNs do you plan on publishing, distributing or representing?

To help us better understand your distribution arrangements which of the following best describes what you *currently* publish

(Select your response)

Nielsen will not pass your details on to any third party organisation; your information is only available to book buyers subscribing to one of our information services and only if they wish to set up a trading relationship with you. You may be contacted by our Editorial team to help set the service up or if there are questions relating to your bibliographic data.

As a client of Nielsen Book Services Ltd, we will contact you, as and when appropriate, to ensure you are fully informed of any relevant service information: up-dates, enhancements, product maintenance etc. These communications will cover both free and subscription based services and any impact on your service or your title records, including changes in government legislation, as well as other relevant and appropriate information.

Nielsen Book would also like to keep you informed of our latest news, forthcoming events and relevant industry updates via our marketing communications (newsletters and as appropriate new services and enhancements that might be relevant to your organization). Please tick this box if you would like to receive marketing information from Nielsen Book Services Ltd in the future.

Send in details >   Cancel Registration

Complete the form, making sure that you use the same details you submitted when registering to purchase your ISBN numbers. This will ensure that Nielsen can match your Title Editor account with the correct publishing imprint. Note that all fields are mandatory. When completed, click **SEND IN DETAILS** at the bottom of the page.

Your account will take 5-10 working days to process. Once set up, Nielsen Book Services will email you login details for your account.

Step 4:

nielsen

Home | About Us | Contact Us | Send Message

Nielsen Title Editor
For publishers, including self-published authors, distributors and sales representatives worldwide. Manage your title data on the Nielsen Book database.

Log in

User name

Help I've forgotten my user name

Password

Help I've forgotten my password

Log in »

After your account has been set up, return to the Title Editor website and click **LOG IN** where you can then enter the login details emailed to you.

Step 5:

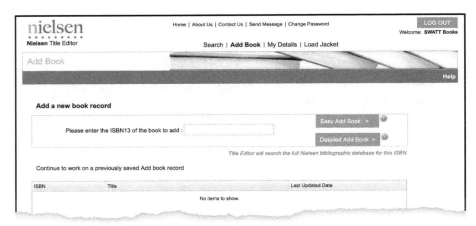

Once logged in, you will come to your Title Editor Dashboard. Click **ADD BOOK** from the menu at the top of the page.

Step 6:

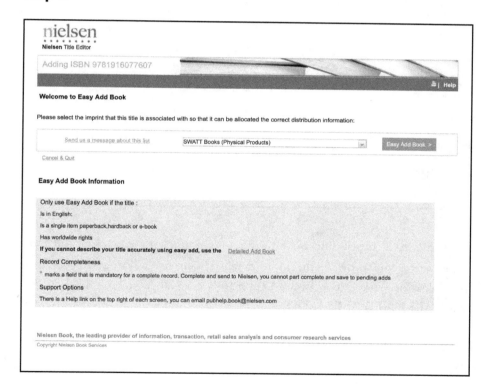

Enter in the ISBN number of the print edition of your book and click **EASY ADD BOOK** .

Step 7:

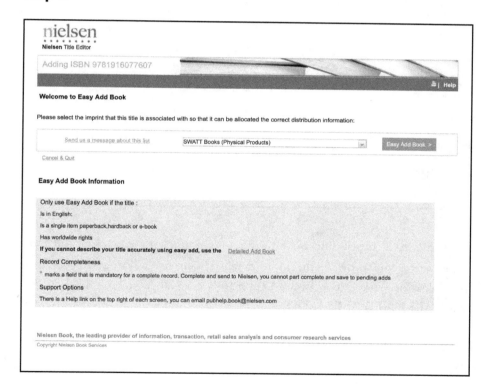

Next, select your Imprint from the pull-down menu, and then click **EASY ADD BOOK** .

Step 8:

Now fill in as much information about your book as you can. The more information you provide, the more detailed your book listing will be. Note that all fields marked with a blue * are mandatory. When you are finished click **SUBMIT RECORD TO NIELSEN'S** .

Step 9:

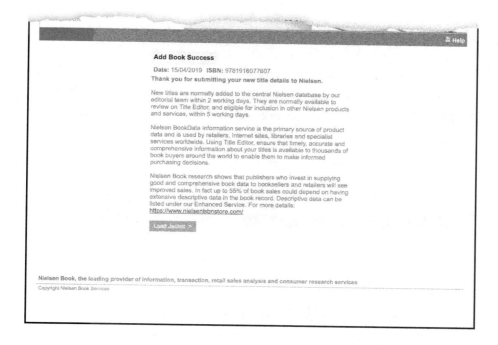

After submitting the book record, you will be presented with a confirmation screen. Next click on **LOAD JACKET** at the bottom of the page.

Step 10:

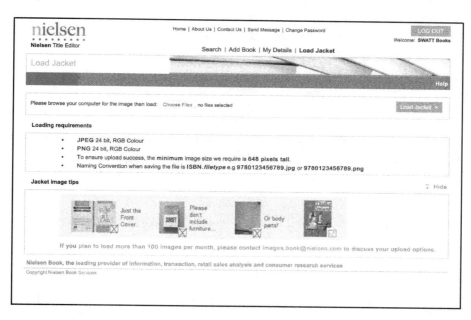

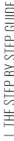

In the Load Jacket page, choose the JPEG file of your book cover. I recommend using the one you used for your eBook cover as this will be the best quality and already compliant with Nielsen's specifications. Note that you will need to change the name of this file to the ISBN number of the book so that Nielsen's can match the cover artwork to the correct listing. Once selected, click **LOAD JACKET** .

Once the jacket artwork has successfully loaded, you will see a confirmation message appear at the top of the screen

And that's it. It will take about 5-10 business days for the listing to be approved by Nielsen's and added to the International Book Database.

Chapter 7

"Published" is not the end of the story

Marketing

You could be forgiven for thinking that now your book is published and available for readers to buy, that is the end of the story. I'm sorry to say that nothing could be further from the truth. "Publishing" your book is just the beginning of your journey as a published author. Now the never-ending job of marketing and promoting your book begins.

As a self-published author, you are responsible for the success or failure of your book and taking a "Write it and they will come" attitude will almost guarantee that it is the latter. But don't worry, with a little ingenuity and outside-the-box thinking, the task of promoting your book can be interesting and rewarding, and you never know, you might find that you enjoy it.

Even though I do have several years of marketing experience in my chequered past, I would by no means class myself as an expert in book marketing. I'm going to touch briefly on some of the basic ways that you can market and promote your book as a means to get you started. But if you want a more professional insight from someone who really knows what they are talking about, I recommend you pick up a copy of *Book Marketing Made Simple* by my good friend Karen Williams.

Your author website

The first, and most obvious, marketing tool you can use is to organise setting up an author website. It is super easy to build a good quality Wordpress website for very little investment. It is entirely possible to sign up for a site fully hosted by Wordpress using their domain completely for free. However, as with the rest of this journey, I would recommend investing a bit of money to do it properly. I would suggest that you register for your own domain name (which ranges from £5-£20 per year), and opt for your own hosting service, which you can commonly get from the same company from whom you registered the domain. When I previously ran a Wordpress website for my agency, the domain and hosting (including unlimited storage and up to 50 email addresses) cost just over £160 a year from 1and1.co.uk.

Wordpress is by far the best option for authors who don't have any web design experience, as it gives you a great-looking site that you have full control over without needing to know or learn any code. Plus, many of the Wordpress themes support e-commerce plugins, so you can sell your book directly off your website without having to send your readers to Amazon.

"What do I include on my author website?" I hear you ask. Well, a full author bio is a great place to start. Tell your readers who you are, what you do and what motivated you to become a writer. Talk about your passions, and maybe show them where you love to write; really let your readers in so that they can form a more personal connection with you.

Next, you want to have a page about your book(s). Give a more in-depth introduction to the book than what is limited to appearing on the back cover and talk about why you wrote this particular book. Maybe even include a brief excerpt from the book to draw in new readers.

If you're going to be running any events related to your book(s), such as book signings, speaking engagements or interviews, then you should also include an events calendar page. Let your readers know what you're up to and where, so that if they want to meet you, they can. Possibly include a wider range of writing and book-related events, as this will help foster a sense of community and help single you out as an author of influence in your area.

Lastly, you need to include a contact page. This can either be a listing of your email address and/or phone number, or if you want to feel a little bit more in control of who you communicate with, you can set up a contact form that readers fill in if they want to get in touch with you. The completed form information is then sent to you via email and then it is up to you how and if you reply.

Social media

The next big marketing tool you should use as an author is a presence on social media. There is a whole raft of platforms out there to choose from –Facebook, Twitter, Instagram, Pinterest, LinkedIn, the list keeps growing. There are no hard and fast rules as to which ones you should be on, but my advice is to try out a few and see how you get on with them. Experiment to see what works and what doesn't. After a while, it will become clear which is the best platform(s) for you and you can then slowly weed out the ones that don't work for you, or that you just don't enjoy using.

One key thing to remember about social media is that consistency is king. If you are going to be on social media, you need to post regularly. Figuring out what to post can sometimes be difficult but posting quality content on a consistent basis is the key to building a loyal and *engaged* tribe of fans. I emphasise engaged because it is, in my opinion, the strongest indicator of whether social media activity is working or not. Just having a thousand people following you is not enough; you need those people to be engaged with you by liking, sharing and commenting on your content.

Many people find social media a tough nut to crack, and I freely admit I find it a difficult area in which to succeed. But when it works, it can get you and your book in front of people from right around the world that you are unlikely to be able to reach in any other way.

Book launch

A book launch can be a fantastic opportunity to start your journey as a published author with a bang. It is basically a party celebrating your achievement and can be as low-key or elaborate as you wish (or your wallet can afford). There is a huge amount of planning and logistics that needs to go into a successful book launch, such as:

> Choosing a venue, date, and time

> Deciding whether to offer drinks and/or nibbles. If so, is it an open bar or pay for?

> Writing out a guest list and sending invitations. Obviously, you want friends and family there, but don't forget about the press, book critics and influential members of your target audience.

> Make sure you have enough copies of your book on hand if you are going to be selling or giving it away on the day, plus have a method of taking payment if you're going to be selling.

> Plenty of pens for book signings ☺

> And make sure that your book is available to buy from retailers either by the day or very shortly afterwards with a firm on-sale date confirmed. That way the buzz generated by your launch can translate into online book sales immediately.

Press releases & general PR

Not everyone who you want to know about your book is going to come to your launch event, but you still need to make them aware that your book has been published. This is where sending out press releases to the media comes in but doesn't just stop with announcing that your book has gone on sale. Think outside the box and shout about any milestone you or your book reaches. X number of copies sold, made the Amazon bestseller list, awards for you or your book, anniversaries, second editions and so on can all be great news stories for your book.

Research a list of local and national press contacts who would be interested in hearing about your book and start sending them press releases. Don't bombard them but keep them abreast of what you have been doing. Make sure that the releases themselves are good quality and have enough content in them to reduce the amount of work the journalist needs to do in order to print your story. Making it easier for them will make it more likely that they will include you.

If you have the budget available, I would consider approaching a PR agency with experience in book promotion who can guide you on who you need to contact and what you should be sending them. A great agency I wholeheartedly recommend is Bookollective: http://www.bookollective.com. They have helped to secure some fantastic coverage for a number of my clients, both on a local and national level.

If you are on a bit of a budget and want some help with a more DIY approach, I suggest you pick up a copy of Paul Blanchard's book *Fast PR*. It's jam-packed with hard-hitting, no-nonsense advice on how to conduct PR like the pros.

Author appearances

Author appearance can take many forms: holding a book signing or reading at a local bookstore; interviews on TV or radio; or being a guest speaker at a conference or event. This sort of publicity is not for everyone. If you're a bit of an introvert who prefers to write as opposed to speaking, then you may find these types of public appearances very stressful and not overly enjoyable. However, if you can overcome your stage fright and get accustomed to speaking in public, author appearances can greatly increase your profile and allow your readers to interact with you directly. Not to mention that these sorts of events are tailor-made for selling; just make sure that you bring a few boxes of books with you along with a method of taking payment and a pen for signings.

Pay Per Click advertising

The last marketing tool I'm going to touch on is Pay Per Click (PPC) advertising. PPC is a digital advertising model that drives traffic to a specific location. You pay a small fee for every person who clicks on your ad. This sort of advertising started out on first-tier search engines like Google and Bing but is now available on all major social media platforms.

PPC advertising can be very effective, as you can be extremely specific on who you target to see your ads, and you are in complete control over your budget (usually by setting a maximum spend per day). However, it can take a bit of trial and error to find the right combination of image, heading and ad copy that entices people to click on your ad. You also need to make sure that the page you send people who click on your ad to is optimised to convert the curious clicker into a buyer. This trial and error can take time, all of which could be costing you in unconverted clicks, but I know of many authors who swear by it.

If you want further help and advice around PPC, I would recommend having a conversation with Bold Internet: http://www.boldinternet.com (for search engine PPC), or Marketing With Ethics: https://marketingwithethics.com (for social media PPC). I have worked with both agencies and they really know their stuff.

***

There are obviously far more marketing strategies and channels out there than what I have covered here. But this at least gives you a starting point to help you build some sales, which will allow you to invest in further marketing opportunities. The important thing is to do *something*, and don't be afraid to think outside the box.

Second editions & reprints

One thing no one tells you when you set out to write a book is that it is never finished. There will always be room for improvement; you may spot a mistake that somehow slipped through all the checks; new information may come to light; you may have changed your position on a particular subject; or your writing style may have improved.

There can be many reasons for you wanting to re-release your book, and yes it can mean subjecting yourself to a condensed version of the publishing process again, but this time you will know what you are doing and it will be easier. Also, second editions offer the opportunity to breathe new life into your book if sales have plateaued or started to drop off. I know of many authors who will produce a second edition of their book without changing a thing except for the cover art. It gives you the opportunity to repeat some or all of the media hype and promotion you did when you published the first edition.

Difference between second editions and reprints

It is important to know if you are going to make changes to your book what constitutes a second edition and what is simply a reprint.

A reprint will have exactly the same ISBN number, the same cover, and for the most part, the same content and artwork. Reprints are reserved for correcting typos and minor mistakes that slipped through all the proofing first time around – and don't worry, this happens all the time so don't beat yourself up! This can be spelling or grammatical errors, or minor corrections such as an image in the wrong location or incorrect references. Anything that does not alter the fundamental content of the book can be done under the definition of a reprint.

The process for a reprint is very simple: just make the corrections required to both the print and the eBook artwork, then upload the new artwork files to your existing book listing on Amazon KDP and Ingram Spark. That's it. The new artwork will take around 14 days to update on all the retail channels where your book is listed, but after that point when anyone orders a copy of your book it will be printed using the new artwork.

Second editions, on the other hand, are rather more complex. If you need to make significant changes to the content, such as rewriting sections, adding new content or deleting old content, that constitutes a requirement for a second edition under the terms of your ISBN number. You need to apply a new set of ISBN numbers to your print and eBook editions and then publish them as completely new listings, going through the publishing process again starting from page 110.

Switching to traditional publishing

The final thing that I want to leave you with are my thoughts on using self-publishing as a springboard to securing a traditional publishing deal. In the introduction to this book, I discussed how difficult it can be to get a book deal from a traditional publisher. If that is still your ultimate dream, don't despair. There is an increasing trend of successful self-published books being picked up by traditional publishing houses.

If your self-published book starts to gain some real traction and breaks into bestseller lists beyond its niche genre, then there is the possibility that a publishing house will approach you. It's a slim possibility and requires your book to make plenty of noise in terms of both sales and publicity, but it does happen… just look at what happened with *The Martian* by Andy Weir.

The most likely scenario is that after your book has accumulated some decent sales figures and some killer reviews, you then start pitching your book to publishers as you might have done in the beginning. The difference now is that your book is no longer an unknown risk to the publisher. You can prove to them that the book has a market through your sales to date, marketing activity, reviews and social media following. It weighs the decision of the publisher more towards concerns of "Does this book fit with our brand?" as opposed to "Are we going to be able to sell this book?"

Now don't get me wrong, securing a traditional book deal off the back of self-publishing is still a long and difficult slog. You are still going to have to deal with plenty of rejection letters. However, if/when that acceptance letter comes in, you will be in a much stronger position at the bargaining table when it comes to negotiating your contract than you would have been if you had approached them with just a manuscript. They now have something to lose, because the sales of your book are no longer an unknown, as you already have a proven sales history for the book. You still need to be mindful during the negotiations of just what you are giving up; you will be signing the rights to your book over to someone else and with it control as well as the majority of your royalties, so make sure that what you are getting back in terms of an advance and commitment from the publisher is worth it.

Conclusion

Before I leave you, there is one last thing that I want to touch on, and that is the impact that self-publishing has had on the publishing industry as a whole.

Like many radical changes in history, self-publishing is seen in many different lights depending on your opinion. People either love it or loathe it. They tout it as either the destruction of the publishing industry or the route to writers' utopia! I exaggerate of course, but you get the drift.

I want to take a minute to explore the two sides of that divide as it has appeared in the media and weigh in with my take on the matter.

The destruction of the publishing industry

Change in any industry can be a scary thing for most people to accept, which inevitably leads to resistance and backlash. The shift toward self-publishing is no exception.

Take Ros Barber for example. Ros is an author with a long career in traditional publishing, who in 2016 wrote an article for the Guardian newspaper[1] in which she said,

---

[1] https://www.theguardian.com/books/booksblog/2016/mar/21/for-me-traditional-publishing-means-poverty-but-self-publish-no-way

"You risk looking like an amateur … Good writers need even better editors. They need brilliant cover designers. They need imaginative marketers and well-connected publicists. All these things are provided by a traditional publisher, and what's more, it doesn't cost you a penny. They pay you! If a self-published author wants to avoid looking like an amateur, they'd better be prepared to shell out some serious cash to get professional help in all the areas where they don't excel. And I mean serious."

Then you have renowned book critic Ron Charles, who submitted an open letter to the Washington Post[2] titled "No, I Don't Want to Read your Self-Published Book", in which he cited concerns that there were too many self-published authors, and that self-published books lacked quality, and were published by authors with little understanding of their audience or the market.

Or this quote from professional blogger Tom Jager in an article for Independent Publishing Magazine[3]:

"The market is suffocated with worthless literature, and self-publishing contributes towards that mess."

Not to mention that a brief skim through the various writers' forums will uncover a plethora of general opinion from authors and writing enthusiasts alike, such as this response to a question on Bayt[4]:

"Few things can be as frustrating as self-publishing. The chances of (success) for any starting writer are minimal, and even more reduced if he decides to self-publish."

2   https://www.washingtonpost.com/news/arts-and-entertainment/wp/2014/10/01/no-i-dont-want-to-read-your-self-published-book/?utm_term=.ea88b7c37100)
3   http://www.theindependentpublishingmagazine.com/2016/06/the-main-problems-for-self-published-authors-tom-jager-guest-post.html
4   https://www.bayt.com/en/specialties/q/305907/what-is-your-opinion-on-self-publishing-are-these-books-not-as-good-as-books-from-publishing-houses/

The route to writers' utopia

As with any polarising subject, for every naysayer, you have the flipside of the coin, people singing its praises. Such as best-selling author and blogger Kristin Lamb who in a blog response[5] to Ros Barber's article, said:

> *"Self-published authors have largely been responsible for many of the most beneficial changes in publishing history."*

Or novelist Louise Walters who is quoted as saying in an interview with the Guardian newspaper[6]:

> *"Footing the bill to bring out the book means the responsibility is on my shoulders, but at the same time it's incredibly freeing. I can market this book in any way I choose; I have real input into every decision regarding my work; I'll even earn a fairer share of the proceeds from each sale … It's only a book, after all, and self-publishing is a whole lot of fun."*

Carlos Harrison quoted Hugh Howey, author of Wool, in an article in the Miami Herald[7] as saying:

> *"With self-publishing you don't waste your time trying to get published, which can take years of query letters and agenting, and all this stuff. You go straight to the real gatekeepers, which are the readers. If they respond favourably and you have sales, you can leverage that into a writing career. If they don't, you write the next thing. Either way you're not spending your time trying to get published, you're spending your time writing the next work."*

---

5   http://authorkristenlamb.com/2016/04/real-writers-dont-self-publish
6   https://www.theguardian.com/books/booksblog/2016/feb/22/i-didnt-want-to-resort-to-self-publishing-but-its-an-exhilarating-change
7   http://www.miamiherald.com/latest-news/article1944481.html

CONCLUSION

185

You also find champions of self-publishing in the same authors' forums, such as Olivia Lynn Jarmusch and her fantastic response to a Q&A question on Goodreads[8]:

> *"I think self-publishing is a great option for just getting started and building your platform! It helps you walk through the entire process of creating, editing, finishing, publishing, and promoting your book, and you learn SO much through it!"*

The missing opinion

One opinion that is suspiciously missing from the debate is that of the big publishing houses. In all my reading on the subject, I have yet to come across a sitting senior exec from any of the big 5 publishers going on record about their views on the boom in self-publishing. My gut feeling is that the Penguins and the Random Houses of the industry either are ignoring it in the hope that it will go away, which is unlikely, or they simply are taking the view that is it beneath them to worry about. They probably think that if a good book comes out of self-publishing then they can just approach the author directly with a book deal safe in the knowledge that the book has already proven itself. Which is exactly what happened with *Fifty Shades of Grey*, *The Martian*, and *The Celestine Prophecy*.

My opinion of self-publishing

As someone who makes their living helping authors self-publish, my opinions on the matter should be pretty obvious. But I do agree with some of the points made by those who are fighting against the trend. There ARE loads of poor quality self-published books out there. Just because you can self-publish your book with just a few clicks of a mouse doesn't necessarily mean that you should.

I think Louise Walters really hits the nail on the head with her comment about taking responsibility for her books' success. If you truly believe in your book, invest in it! Yes, it is a considerable investment, but it doesn't need to be the extortionate investment that Ros Barber would lead you to believe. Choosing the right editors, designers and other author support partners is important and can make the difference between your book being a success and you enjoying the process, and you becoming bitter and disillusioned at becoming a writer and giving up on your dream.

In closing I would also like to add that I don't view self-publishing as being black or white, good or bad. I see it as being many shades of grey (probably around fifty ☺) in how appropriate it is for each individual author and their particular situation.

***

So, there you have it; the self-publishing process distilled into a (hopefully) easy to understand primer that will give you the necessary tools and understanding to enter the world of publishing on your own two feet.

You may have arrived at the end of this book filled with a sense of being overwhelmed at just what is involved in self-publishing your book – and that's OK. It's perfectly normal to feel that way. It IS a huge amount of work, but the rewards far outweigh the effort.

Think of the immense feeling of satisfaction you will feel holding your book in your hand for the first time. The overwhelming sense of pride you will feel when you see your book on sale in places like Amazon, Waterstones or Barnes & Noble. The vast sense of achievement that you have been able to make a difference to someone's life the first time you read a review for your book. All of these things make the journey worthwhile.

Need help?

First of all, I want to thank you personally for taking the time to read this through to the very end. From the feedback that I have had for this book so far, I'm guessing that you are feeling one of three things…

One: You're really excited about the possibilities that self-publishing has to offer you as an author, and you can't want to get started.

Two: You are feeling empowered by the possibilities of self-publishing but are having doubts as to whether you have the time or the patience to implement everything you've read in this book.

Three: You are feeling a bit like a deer caught in headlights at how much there is to do, think about, and implement, but at the same time you don't want to miss the opportunity.

If either of the last two scenarios sound like how you are feeling right now, I'm here to help. There are several packages that I offer authors to help them through the self-publishing process, depending on how involved you need/want me to be.

Package 1: Consultation

If you're confident about undertaking the work yourself, but just need a bit of support along the way, then this package is for you. In it you will have access to me throughout your publishing journey, to guide you on what your next steps are and what you need to be thinking about.

Package 2: Consultation + Design

With this package, you get everything from Package 1, plus I will design and typeset your book for you. You will receive print-ready artwork as well as the required EPub files ready for you to publish.

Package 3: All-Inclusive Solution

This last package is an all singing and dancing solution that will take you from final manuscript all the way through to your book being on sale worldwide, using the processes that I have outlined in this book. It includes:

> Editing
> Design & typesetting
> eBook conversion
> Registration of your publishing accounts
> Purchase of your ISBN numbers
> Listing of your book in both print and eBook with both Amazon and Ingram Spark
> Legal deposits
> And a free file copy of your print edition

It is important to note that I walk what I talk and with this package you will retain 100% of your copyrights and keep 100% of your royalties too.

If you want to know more about the support I can offer you as an author, please visit my website at www.swatt-books.co.uk, or book a one-to-one consultation with me via my online diary at www.youcanbookme.swattbooks.com.

Resources

Here is a list of websites that you might find very useful during your journey to becoming a published author.

Ingram Spark – https://www.ingramspark.com
Leading international PoD self-publishing platform.

Nielsen UK ISBN Agency – http://www.isbn.nielsenbook.co.uk
ISBN Agency for the United Kingdom and Ireland.

Nielsen ISBN Store – https://www.nielsenisbnstore.com
Portal to purchase ISBN numbers for books published in the United Kingdom and Ireland.

Nielsen Title Editor – https://www.nielsentitleeditor.com/titleeditor/
Portal for submission of title information for books published in the United Kingdom and Ireland to the International Book Database.

International ISBN Agency – https://www.isbn-international.org
Central government body for ISBN number allocation worldwide.

Worldwide ISBN Agency Database –
https://www.isbn-international.org/agencies
Database managed by the International ISBN Agency which lists all official ISBN agencies worldwide.

Kindle Direct Publishing – https://kdp.amazon.com/en_US/
Publishing platform for Amazon.

British Library Legal Deposits – https://www.bl.uk/legal-deposit
Information regarding legal deposit requirements to the British Library.

Agency for the Legal Deposit Libraries – https://www.legaldeposit.org.uk
Agency website for the additional legal deposit libraries in the United Kingdom.

The Alliance of Independent Authors –
https://www.allianceindependentauthors.org
International organisation supporting self-published authors.

BIC Subject Categories List – https://ns.editeur.org/bic_categories
List of subject categories and qualifiers for the BIC book classification system
used by Ingram Spark:

Thema Subject Categories List – https://ns.editeur.org/thema/en
List of subject categories and qualifiers for the Thema book classification system,
which is soon to replace the BIC system.

Authors' Licencing & Collection Society (ALCS) – https://www.alcs.co.uk
Non-profit membership organisation that collects royalties for secondary uses of
books and published materials on behalf of authors.

PLR (Public Lending Rights) – https://www.bl.uk/plr
British Library portal allowing authors to register for the PLR scheme which
entitles authors to payment from the British Government for books borrowed
from public libraries.

Bowker – http://www.bowker.com/products/ISBN-US.html
ISBN agency for the United States of America

Authors Journey Facebook Group –
https://www.facebook.com/groups/authorsjourney
Facebook group that supports and inspires independent authors.

Librotas – https://librotas.com
Book mentoring and publishing services from Karen Williams; primarily aimed
at business authors, but also has many resources that would benefit all types of
authors, such as marketing advice and writing challenges.

Bookollective – http://www.bookollective.com

Book PR and marketing agency who specialise in press releases, media targeting, social media support, launch event planning as well as arranging blog tours and book reviews.

Step by Step Listening – https://stepbysteplistening.com

Sheryl Andrews is a clarity and confidence coach and is really great at helping authors to manage their critic and get past any mental blocks that might be affecting their ability to complete their books.

Fast PR: Give Yourself a Huge Media Boost, by Paul Blanchard – https://www.amazon.co.uk/Fast-PR-Yourself-Media-Boost/dp/1911443046

This book is a great do-it-yourself primer to help you get started with your own PR activities to support your book.

Book Marketing Made Simple, by Karen Williams – https://www.amazon.co.uk/Book-Marketing-Made-Simple-Practical/dp/0995739021

This book is a straightforward guide full of easy-to-follow strategies to market your book at all stages of your journey – from the day you start to write a book until after your book launch.

Jargon buster

Many of these terms you will have seen throughout the book, and others you will come across during your publishing journey.

Barcode: A machine-readable image on the back of a book to indicate the ISBN and sometimes the suggested retail price. Barcodes are often required by many retailers in order to facilitate the sales process.

Copyright: A form of intellectual property (IP), copyright gives the author of an original book exclusive rights to that book's publication, distribution, and adaptation for a certain time period.

Digital Rights Management (DRM): A system or technology used to place restrictions to access or copying of digital content such as eBooks, movies, or music. A publisher or author, not the retailer, determines the level of restrictions applied. This includes how many times content can be downloaded from a single purchase, and the number of devices to which the content can be copied and stored.

Distributor: A party that handles all fulfilment, credit and collections on behalf of a publisher. In the case of the book industry, a distributor would sell to retailers and wholesalers.

E-retailer: An online retailer that sells books, both physical and digital, and often other related merchandise to readers. E-retailers source their products from publishers, wholesalers and distributors but do not have a physical shop space. The biggest e-retailer is Amazon.

Edition: A version of a work. A new edition means that there have been a series of corrections and/or a new feature added (such as a preface, appendix or additional content), or that the content has been revised.

EPub: A format for digital books and publications. EPub allows for the reflowing of content, so that text can be optimized for the display screen and reader preferences being used at the time.

ISBN (International Standard Book Number): A unique 13-digit number provided by your country's ISBN agency and assigned by the publisher to identify a particular format, edition and publisher of a book. ISBNs are used worldwide as a unique identifier for each book title/format combination.

.jpg or .jpeg: An image file format ideal for digital images with large amounts of colour, such as photographs.

Keywords: Single words or short phrases that describe your book and help readers to find your book using a search engine.

Metadata: Details about your title that booksellers and buyers need to know. Metadata includes details specific to a particular form of the book (e.g. price, format, binding type, publication date) as well as general information that may apply to all forms of your book (e.g. author, description, table of contents).

Offset printing: Printing on a traditional printing press where many copies of a book are produced at one time.

On Sale Date: The date to determine when a book may be sold by retail partners. This date can be different from your publication date in order to facilitate a pre-sale period.

Page count: Page count is the total number of pages in the book, including blanks and front matter. The total number of pages must be evenly divisible by 2 in order to allow for correct printing.

PDF: A file format developed by Adobe to allow the creation and sharing of documents that will look and print the same on any computer, monitor, or printer.

Print on Demand (PoD): A type of printing, usually from a digital file to a digital printer. With PoD, the physical book is only printed when it is ordered. The exact number of copies ordered is what is printed. No extra copies are kept on warehouse shelves.

Publication date: The date on which a retail consumer or library may take possession of a book.

Publisher: The entity that owns the legal right to make a book available. They usually also shoulder the burden of the cost of having a book produced.

Retailer: A store that sells books, and often other related merchandise, to readers. Retailers source their products from publishers, wholesalers and distributors.

Returns: Historically, publishers grant booksellers the right to return unwanted and/or overstocked copies of books. These books are considered "returnable." As books are returned, booksellers charge publishers for the cost (i.e. their purchase price) of any books returned and expect to be reimbursed. The cost of returned books is either deducted or netted against the proceeds of book sales of the publisher's titles in the month returns are shipped to the publisher.

Status: Indicates the availability of the book. The book industry uses terms such as forthcoming (going to be published in the future), active (available for purchase now), and publication cancelled (item will not be published now or in the future).

Subject: Subjects are used to categorize books. These categories briefly describe the content of a book. Retailers, distributors, and libraries require you to select at least one subject so that they have an indication of where and how to file a book for reference.

Suggested retail price: Publishers determine the suggested retail list price on the books it publishes for each market. If pricing is not submitted the title will appear as unavailable for sale in that market.

Title: The title information placed is used for all reporting and reseller catalogue communications (where appropriate) and consists of both the main title and any subtitles.

Trade: Refers to traditional bookselling channels, including independent bookstores (e.g. a single store, a local group of stores) and chain bookstores (e.g. Waterstones, Barnes & Noble, Hastings, Books-a-Million).

Track Changes: Is a feature of Microsoft Word where any changes to a manuscript are annotated in a sidebar and tracked for reference.

Trade Discount: An amount or rate by which the cover, list or suggested retail price of an item is reduced when sold to a reseller. The trade discount allows for the reseller to make a profit on the sale of your book.

Widows & orphans: Widows refers to words that appear on their own on a following page (widowed from their associated paragraphs). Orphans refers to a single word that drops onto a line on its own.

Wholesaler: A business that obtains books from publishers and their appointed distributors in order to fulfil orders for retailers and libraries. They offer non-exclusive distribution to publishers. Wholesalers will stock certain quantities of titles but will usually not warehouse your entire inventory. Wholesalers meet customer requests by packaging books across a set of publishers and delivering the goods quickly to meet retailer or library needs.

About the author

Originally born in the UK, Sam Pearce grew up in Toronto Canada where she developed a fascination with art and design by leafing through the album covers of her father's vinyl collection. Despite other passions for music, flying and animals coming and going, the love of design has never gone away.

After a very late change of major in her final year of high school and an extra semester spent as an apprentice in a desktop publishing agency, Sam was accepted to the George Brown College School of Art & Design to study computer graphics and corporate design. After graduation, Sam spent the next 20 years working as a commercial graphic designer in Canada and then in the United Kingdom, after relocating there in 2003.

A fortuitous chain of events saw Sam starting to apply her passion for typography and layout to the art of books in 2012. Several years later another seemingly random event introduced her to the world of self-publishing and the rest, as they say, is history.

Since then, Sam has been involved in the design and publication of over 40 books encompassing a wide range of genres, from business guides and self-help books to children's stories and fantasy fiction. Many books Sam has been involved in have gone onto be nominated and win prestigious awards in their categories as well as topping Amazon bestseller lists.

Sam started SWATT Books as a way of helping independent authors to get their work self-published professionally, affordably and ethically. To give them the opportunity to tell their own stories in their own way and in their own voice without the restrictions and gatekeepers of the traditional publishing world.

CPSIA information can be obtained
at www.ICGtesting.com
Printed in the USA
LVHW101605080519
617104LV00008B/286/P